CW00404610

**TOGAF® 9 Foundation**
Study Guide 2nd Edition

## The Open Group Publications available from Van Haren Publishing

**The TOGAF Series:**
TOGAF® Version 9.1
TOGAF® Version 9.1 – A Pocket Guide
TOGAF® 9 Foundation Study Guide, 2nd Edition
TOGAF® 9 Certified Study Guide, 2nd Edition

**The Open Group Series:**
Cloud Computing for Business – The Open Group Guide
Archimate® 2.0 Specification (Publishes 2012)

**The Open Group Security Series:**
Open Information Security Management Maturity Model (O-ISM3)
Open Enterprise Security Architecture (O-ESA)
Risk Management – The Open Group Guide

All titles are available to purchase from:
www.opengroup.org
www.vanharen.net
and also many international and online distributors.

# TOGAF® 9 Foundation

## Study Guide

## 2nd Edition

**Preparation for the TOGAF 9 Part 1 Examination**

Prepared by Rachel Harrison of Oxford Brookes University

| | |
|---|---|
| Title: | TOGAF® 9 Foundation Study Guide 2nd Edition |
| Subtitle: | Preparation for the TOGAF 9 Part 1 Examination |
| Series: | TOGAF Series |
| A Publication of: | The Open Group |
| Author: | Prof. Rachel Harrison |
| Publisher: | Van Haren Publishing, Zaltbommel, www.vanharen.net |
| ISBN: | 978 90 8753 681 7 |
| Edition: | Second edition, first impression, December 2011 |
| Layout and Cover design: | CO2 Premedia, Amersfoort –NL |
| Print: | Wilco, Amersfoort – NL |
| Copyright: | © 2009-2011 The Open Group. All rights reserved. |

No part of this publication may be reproduced, stored in a retrieval system, or transmitted, in any form or by any means, electronic, mechanical, photocopying, recording, or otherwise, without the prior permission of the copyright owner.

The views expressed in this Study Guide are not necessarily those of any particular member of The Open Group.

In the event of any discrepancy between text in this Study Guide and the official TOGAF documentation, the TOGAF documentation remains the authoritative version for certification, testing by examination, and other purposes. The official TOGAF documentation can be obtained online at www.opengroup.org/togaf.

Document Number: B111

Comments relating to the material contained in this document may be submitted to:

The Open Group
Apex Plaza, Forbury Road
Reading
Berkshire, RG1 1AX
United Kingdom

or by electronic mail to: ogspecs@opengroup.org

For any further enquiries about Van Haren Publishing, please send an email to: info@vanharen.net.

# Contents

# Preface

**This Document**

This document is a Study Guide for TOGAF®9 Foundation. This second edition is based on Version 2 of the TOGAF Certification for People Conformance Requirements, published in December 2011. This edition is aligned to TOGAF Version 9.1, which was published in December 2011.

It gives an overview of every learning objective for the TOGAF 9 Foundation Syllabus and in-depth coverage on preparing and taking the TOGAF 9 Part 1 Examination. It is specifically designed to help individuals prepare for certification.

The audience for this Study Guide is:
- Individuals who require a basic understanding of TOGAF 9
- Professionals who are working in roles associated with an architecture project such as those responsible for planning, execution, development, delivery, and operation
- Architects who are looking for a first introduction to TOGAF 9
- Architects who want to achieve Level 2 certification in a stepwise manner and have not previously qualified as TOGAF 8 Certified

A prior knowledge of enterprise architecture is advantageous but not required. While reading this Study Guide, the reader should also refer to the TOGAF 9 documentation[1] available online at www.opengroup.org/architecture/togaf9-doc/arch and also available in book form.

The Study Guide is structured as shown below. The order of topics corresponds to the learning units of the TOGAF 9 Foundation Syllabus (see Appendix D).
- Chapter 1 (Introduction) provides a brief introduction to TOGAF certification and the TOGAF 9 Part 1 Examination that leads to TOGAF 9 Foundation, as well as how to use this Study Guide.

---

[1] TOGAF Version 9.1 (ISBN is 978 90 8753 679 4 G116), available at www.opengroup.org/bookstore/catalog/g116.htm.

- Chapter 2 (Basic Concepts) introduces the basic concepts of enterprise architecture and TOGAF. This provides a high-level view of TOGAF, enterprise architecture, architecture frameworks, and the contents of TOGAF.
- Chapter 3 (Core Concepts) describes the core concepts of TOGAF 9.
- Chapter 4 (Key Terminology) introduces the key terminology of TOGAF 9.
- Chapter 5 (Introduction to the ADM) introduces the Architecture Development Method (ADM), the objectives of each phase of the ADM, and how to adapt and scope the ADM for use.
- Chapter 6 (The Enterprise Continuum and Tools) describes the Enterprise Continuum and tools; its purpose, and its constituent parts.
- Chapter 7 (The ADM Phases) describes how each of the ADM phases contributes to the success of enterprise architecture.
- Chapter 8 (ADM Guidelines and Techniques) describes guidelines and techniques provided to support application of the ADM.
- Chapter 9 (Architecture Governance) describes Architecture Governance.
- Chapter 10 (Views, Viewpoints, and Stakeholders) introduces the concepts of views and viewpoints and their role in communicating with stakeholders.
- Chapter 11 (Building Blocks) introduces the concept of building blocks.
- Chapter 12 (ADM Deliverables) describes the key deliverables of the ADM cycle and their purpose.
- Chapter 13 (TOGAF Reference Models) describes the TOGAF reference models, including the Technical Reference Model (TRM) and the Integrated Information Infrastructure Reference Model (III-RM).
- Appendix A (Answers to Test Yourself Questions) provides the answers to the Test Yourself sections provided at the end of each chapter.
- Appendix B (Test Yourself Examination Paper) provides a Test Yourself examination to allow you to assess your knowledge of TOGAF and readiness to take the TOGAF 9 Part 1 Examination.
- Appendix C (Test Yourself Examination Paper Answers) provides the answers to the examination in Appendix B.
- Appendix D (TOGAF 9 Foundation Syllabus) provides the TOGAF 9 Foundation Syllabus.

**How to Use this Study Guide**

The chapters in this Study Guide are arranged to follow the organization of the TOGAF 9 Foundation Syllabus (see Appendix D) and should be read in order. However, you may wish to use this Study Guide during review of topics with which you are already familiar, and it is certainly possible to select topics for review in any order. Where a topic requires further information from a later part in the syllabus, a cross-reference is provided.

Within each chapter are "Key Learning Points" and "Summary" sections that help you to easily identify what you need to know for each topic.

Each chapter has a "Test Yourself" questions section that will help you to test your understanding of the chapter and prepare for the TOGAF 9 Part 1 Examination. The purpose of this is to reinforce key learning points in the chapter. These are multiple-choice format questions where you must identify one correct answer.

Each chapter also has a "Recommended Reading" section that indicates the relevant sections in the TOGAF 9 documentation that can be read to obtain a further understanding of the subject material.

Finally, at the end of this Study Guide is a "Test Yourself" examination paper that you can use to test your readiness to take the official TOGAF 9 Part 1 Examination.

### Conventions Used in this Study Guide

The following conventions are used throughout this Study Guide in order to help identify important information and avoid confusion over the intended meaning.

- Ellipsis (…)
  Indicates a continuation; such as an incomplete list of example items, or a continuation from preceding text.
- **Bold**
  Used to highlight specific terms.
- *Italics*
  Used for emphasis. May also refer to other external documents.
- *(Syllabus reference: Unit X, Learning Outcome Y: Statement)*
  Used at the start of a text block to identify the TOGAF 9 Foundation Syllabus learning outcome.

In addition to typographical conventions, the following conventions are used to highlight segments of text:

A Note box is used to highlight useful or interesting information.

A Tip box is used to provide key information that can save you time or that may not be entirely obvious.

## About TOGAF

TOGAF®, an Open Group Standard, is a proven enterprise architecture methodology and framework used by the world's leading organizations to improve business efficiency. It is the most prominent and reliable enterprise architecture standard, ensuring consistent standards, methods, and communication among enterprise architecture professionals. Enterprise architecture professionals fluent in TOGAF standards enjoy greater industry credibility, job effectiveness, and career opportunities. TOGAF helps practitioners avoid being locked into proprietary methods, utilize resources more efficiently and effectively, and realize a greater return on investment.

## About The Open Group

The Open Group is a global consortium that enables the achievement of business objectives through IT standards. With more than 375 member organizations, The Open Group has a diverse membership that spans all sectors of the IT community – customers, systems and solutions suppliers, tool vendors, integrators, and consultants, as well as academics and researchers – to:

- Capture, understand, and address current and emerging requirements, and establish policies and share best practices
- Facilitate interoperability, develop consensus, and evolve and integrate specifications and open source technologies
- Offer a comprehensive set of services to enhance the operational efficiency of consortia
- Operate the industry's premier certification service

Further information on The Open Group is available at www.opengroup.org. The Open Group publishes a wide range of technical documentation, most of which is focused on development of Open Group Standards and Guides, but which also includes white papers, technical studies, certification and testing documentation, and business titles. Full details and a catalog are available at www.opengroup.org/bookstore.

Readers should note that updates – in the form of Corrigenda – may apply to any publication. This information is published at www.opengroup.org/corrigenda.

# About the Author

Rachel Harrison is a Professor of Computer Science in the Department of Computing and Communication Technologies at Oxford Brookes University. Previously she was Professor of Computer Science, Head of the Department of Computer Science, and Director of Research for the School of Systems Engineering at the University of Reading. Her research interests include systems evolution, software metrics, requirements engineering, software architecture, usability, and software testing. She has published over 100 refereed papers and consulted widely with industry, working with organizations such as IBM, the DERA, Philips Research Labs, Praxis Critical Systems, and The Open Group. She is Editor-in-Chief of the Software Quality Journal, published by Springer.

Prof. Harrison holds an MA in Mathematics from Oxford University, an MSc in Computer Science from University College London, and a PhD in Computer Science from the University of Southampton. She is a Member of the British Computer Society, an Affiliate Member of the IEEE-CS, a Member of the Association of Computing Machinery, and is a Chartered Engineer.

# Trademarks

Boundaryless Information Flow™ is a trademark and ArchiMate®, Jericho Forum®, Making Standards Work®, Motif®, OSF/1®, The Open Group®, TOGAF®, UNIX®, and the "X" device are registered trademarks of The Open Group in the United States and other countries.

All other brand, company, and product names are used for identification purposes only and may be trademarks that are the sole property of their respective owners.

# Acknowledgements

The Open Group gratefully acknowledges The Open Group Architecture Forum for developing TOGAF.

The Open Group gratefully acknowledges the following reviewers who participated in the review of this Study Guide:

- Geoff Burke
- Steve Else
- Bill Estrem
- Cathy Fox
- Kyle Gabhart
- Howard Gottlieb
- Paul Holdforth
- Henk Jonkers
- Andrew Josey
- Graham Neal
- Kiichiro Onishi
- Arnold van Overeem
- Andras Szakal
- Robert Weisman
- Ron Widitz

# References

The following documents are referenced in this Study Guide:
- TOGAF Version 9.1, available online at www.opengroup.org/architecture/ togaf9-doc/arch, and also available as TOGAF Version 9.1 "The Book" (ISBN: 978 90 8753 6794) at www.opengroup.org/bookstore/catalog/ g116.htm.
- Why Does Enterprise Architecture Matter?, White Paper by Simon Townson, SAP, November 2008 (W076), published by The Open Group (www.opengroup.org/bookstore/catalog/w076.htm).
- Interoperable Enterprise Business Scenario, October 2002 (K022), published by The Open Group (www.opengroup.org/bookstore/catalog/ k022.htm)
- ISO/IEC 42010:2007, Systems and Software Engineering – Recommended Practice for Architectural Description of Software-Intensive Systems, Edition 1 (technically identical to ANSI/IEEE Std 1471-2000).
- TOGAF Certification for People: Program Summary Datasheet, February 2009, published by The Open Group (www.opengroup.org/togaf9/cert/ docs/togaf9_cert_summary.pdf).
- TOGAF 9 Foundation Datasheet, February 2009, published by The Open Group (www.opengroup.org/togaf9/cert/docs/togaf9_foundation.pdf).
- TOGAF Certification for People: Certification Policy, February 2009 (X091), published by The Open Group (www.opengroup.org/bookstore/ catalog/x091.htm).
- TOGAF Certification for People: Conformance Requirements (Multi-Level), Version 2, December 2011 (X111), published by The Open Group (www.opengroup.org/bookstore/catalog/x111.htm).
- The Clinger-Cohen Act (US Information Technology Management Reform Act 1996).The Sarbanes-Oxley Act (US Public Company Accounting Reform and Investor Protection Act 2002).
- EU Directives on the Award of Public Contracts
- Bill Estrem, "TOGAF to the Rescue" (www.opengroup.org/downloads)

The following web links are referenced in this Study Guide:
- The Open Group TOGAF 9 Certification web site: www.opengroup.org/ togaf9/cert
- The TOGAF information web site: www.togaf.info

# Chapter 1

# Introduction

## 1.1 Key Learning Points

This document is a Study Guide for TOGAF® Version 9 for students planning to become certified for TOGAF 9 Foundation. It will familiarize you with all the topics that you need to know in order to pass the TOGAF 9 Part 1 Examination.

It gives an overview of every learning objective for the TOGAF 9 Foundation Syllabus and in-depth coverage on preparing and taking the TOGAF 9 Part 1 Examination. It is specifically designed to help individuals prepare for certification.

This first chapter will familiarize you with the TOGAF 9 certification program and its principles, as well as give you important information about the structure of the TOGAF 9 Part 1 Examination.

The objectives of this chapter are as follows:
- To provide an understanding of TOGAF certification and why you should become certified
- To learn key facts about the TOGAF 9 Part 1 Examination

## 1.2 The TOGAF Certification for People Program

*(Syllabus Reference: Unit 13, Learning Outcome 1: You should be able to briefly explain the TOGAF Certification program, and distinguish between the levels for certification.)*

Certification is available to individuals who wish to demonstrate they have attained the required knowledge and understanding of TOGAF Version 9.[2]

---

2    This second edition of this Study Guide has been updated to cover Version 2 of the TOGAF Certification for People Conformance Requirements, which are aligned to TOGAF Version 9.1.

There are two levels defined for TOGAF 9 People certification, denoted Level 1 and Level 2, which lead to certification at TOGAF 9 Foundation and TOGAF 9 Certified, respectively. This Study Guide covers the first of these – TOGAF 9 Foundation. Studying for TOGAF 9 Foundation can be used as a learning objective towards achieving TOGAF 9 Certified, as the learning outcomes in TOGAF 9 Foundation are also required in TOGAF 9 Certified.

Table 1:    Certification Levels and and Associated Labels

| Certification Level | Certification Label |
| --- | --- |
| Level 1 | TOGAF 9 Foundation |
| Level 2 | TOGAF 9 Certified |

**Why is TOGAF certification important?**

The existence of a certification program for TOGAF provides a strong incentive for organizations to standardize on TOGAF as the open method for enterprise architecture, and so avoid lock-in to proprietary methods. It is an important step in making enterprise architecture a well-recognized discipline, and in introducing rigor into the procurement of tools and services for enterprise architecture.

The two certification levels are summarized in Figure 1 and Figure 2. Figure 1 shows the relationship between Level 1 and Level 2. Level 2 (TOGAF 9 Certified) is a superset of the requirements for Level 1 (TOGAF 9 Foundation).[3]

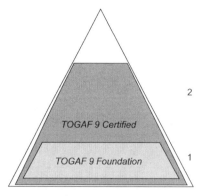

Figure 1:    TOGAF 9 Certification Program Overview

---

3    The gap at the top of the pyramid is to signify that additional certification levels may be added in the future.

The Open Group also provides a certification path direct to Level 2 (TOGAF 9 Certified) for individuals who have previously achieved the TOGAF 8 Certified qualification. This is known as the bridging option and is illustrated in Figure 2.

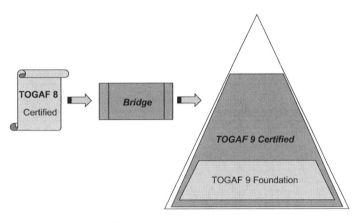

Figure 2:    Bridging TOGAF 8 to TOGAF 9

### 1.2.1  Certification Document Structure

The documents available to support the program are as shown in Figure 3.

Program description documents, such as this Study Guide, are intended for an end-user audience including those interested in becoming certified. The Program definition documents are intended for trainers, examination developers, and the Certification Authority. All these documents are available from The Open Group web site.[4]

**Why become certified?**

Becoming certified demonstrates clearly to employers and peers your commitment to enterprise architecture as a discipline. In particular, it demonstrates that you possess a body of core knowledge about TOGAF as an open, industry standard framework and method for enterprise architecture. The Open Group publishes the definitive directory of TOGAF Certified individuals, and certified service and product offerings, and issues certificates.

---

4    For the latest information on examinations, see the TOGAF 9 Certification web site at www.opengroup.org/togaf9/cert.

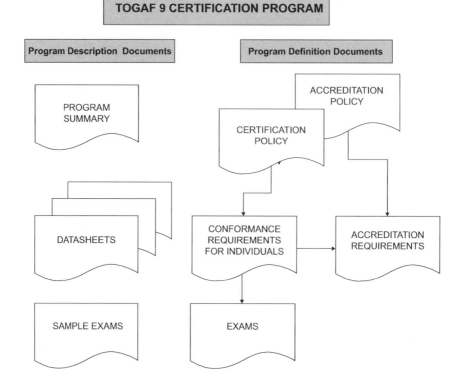

Figure 3:    Certification Document Structure

## 1.2.2  Program Vision and Principles

The vision for the program is to define and promote a market-driven education and certification program to support TOGAF 9. The program has been designed with the following principles in mind:

Table 2:    TOGAF Certification Principles

| Principle | Certification Aspects |
|---|---|
| Openness | The program is open to applicants from all countries. |
| Fairness | Certification is achieved only by passing an examination that is equivalent to that taken by any other candidate. |
| Market Relevance | The program is structured to meet the needs of the market for conversion from TOGAF 8, as well as for people without prior TOGAF certification, and for certification at two levels. Additional levels may be introduced during the life of the program, as may updated versions of TOGAF. |

| Principle | Certification Aspects |
|---|---|
| Learning Support | Training courses are provided by third parties, according to the needs of the market. |
| Quality | Training course providers may choose to seek Open Group accreditation for their courses. Accredited courses are listed on The Open Group web site. |
| Best Practice | The program is designed to follow industry best practice for equivalent certification programs. |

### 1.2.3   TOGAF 9 Foundation

The purpose of certification to TOGAF 9 Level 1, known as TOGAF 9 Foundation, is to provide validation that the candidate has gained an acceptable level of knowledge of the terminology, structure, and basic concepts of TOGAF 9, and understands the core principles of enterprise architecture and TOGAF.

The learning objectives at this level focus on knowledge and comprehension.

Individuals certified at this level will have demonstrated their understanding of:
- The basic concepts of enterprise architecture and TOGAF
- The core concepts of TOGAF 9
- The key terminology of TOGAF 9
- The ADM cycle and the objectives of each phase, and how to adapt and scope the ADM
- The concept of the Enterprise Continuum; its purpose, and its constituent parts
- How each of the ADM phases contributes to the success of enterprise architecture
- The ADM guidelines and techniques
- How Architecture Governance contributes to the Architecture Development Cycle
- The concepts of views and viewpoints and their role in communicating with stakeholders
- The concept of building blocks
- The key deliverables of the ADM cycle
- The TOGAF reference models
- The TOGAF certification program

**Examination**

Certification for TOGAF 9 Foundation is achieved by passing the TOGAF 9 Part 1 Examination. This is a multiple-choice examination with 40 questions.[5]

**What is the relationship between TOGAF 9 Foundation and TOGAF 9 Certified?**

The learning outcomes for TOGAF 9 Foundation are a subset of those for TOGAF 9 Certified. Candidates are able to choose whether they wish to become certified in a stepwise manner by starting with TOGAF 9 Foundation and then at a later date TOGAF 9 Certified, or alternately to go direct to TOGAF 9 Certified by taking the combined examination.

### 1.2.4 The Certification Process

This Study Guide is aimed at preparing you to become certified for TOGAF 9 Foundation. The examination for this level is the TOGAF 9 Part 1 Examination, which comprises 40 multiple-choice questions.

The TOGAF 9 Foundation Syllabus for the examination is contained in Appendix D. Certain topic areas are weighted as more important than others and thus have more questions. The 11 topic areas covered by the examination together with the number of questions per area in the examination follows:

1. Basic Concepts (3 questions)
2. Core Concepts (3 questions)
3. Introduction to the ADM (3 questions)
4. The Enterprise Continuum and Tools (4 questions)
5. ADM Phases (9 questions)
6. ADM Guidelines and Techniques (6 questions)
7. Architecture Governance (4 questions)
8. Architecture Views, Viewpoints, and Stakeholders (2 questions)
9. Building Blocks (2 questions)
10. ADM Deliverables (2 questions)
11. TOGAF Reference Models (2 questions)

---

5   For the latest information on examinations, see the TOGAF 9 Certification web site at www.opengroup.org/togaf9/cert.

*1.2.4.1  Format of the Examination Questions*

The examination questions are multiple-choice questions. These are very similar in format to the Test Yourself questions included in each chapter. Note that the exact format for display is test center-specific and will be made clear on the screens when taking the examination.

**Exam Tip**

Please read each question carefully before reading the answer options. Be aware that some questions may seem to have more than one right answer, but you are to look for the one that makes the most sense and is the most correct.

*1.2.4.2  What do I need to bring with me to take the Examination?*

You should consult with the test center regarding the forms of picture ID you are required to bring with you to verify your identification.

*1.2.4.3  Can I refer to materials while I take the Examination?*

No; it is a closed-book examination.

*1.2.4.4  If I fail, how soon can I retake the Examination?*

You should consult the current policy on The Open Group web site. At the time of writing, the policy states that individuals who have failed the examination are not allowed to retake the examination within one (1) month of the first sitting.

## 1.2.5  Preparing for the Examination

You can prepare for the examination by working through this Study Guide section-by-section. A mapping of the sections of this Study Guide to the TOGAF 9 Foundation Syllabus is given in Appendix D. After completing each section, you should answer the Test Yourself questions and read the referenced sections from the TOGAF documentation. Once you have completed all the sections in this Study Guide, you can then attempt the Test Yourself examination paper in Appendix B. This is designed to give a thorough test of your knowledge. If you have completed all the prescribed preparation and can attain a pass mark for the Test Yourself examination paper as described in Appendix C, then it is likely you are ready to sit the examination.

## 1.3  Summary

The TOGAF 9 People certification program is a knowledge-based certification program. It has two levels, Level 1 and Level 2, which lead to certification for TOGAF 9 Foundation and TOGAF 9 Certified, respectively.

The topic for this Study Guide is preparation for taking the TOGAF 9 Part 1 Examination that leads to the TOGAF 9 Foundation certification. The examination comprises 40 simple multiple-choice questions to be completed in one hour.[6]

Preparing for the examination includes the following steps:
- You should work through this Study Guide step-by-step.
- At the end of each chapter, you should complete the Test Yourself questions and read the sections of the TOGAF documentation listed under Recommended Reading.
- Once you have completed all the chapters in this Study Guide, you should attempt the Test Yourself examination paper given in Appendix C.
- If you can attain the target score in Appendix D, then you have completed your preparation.

## 1.4  Test Yourself Questions

Q1:   How many certification levels are there in the TOGAF 9 People certification program?
   A.  1
   B.  2
   C.  3
   D.  4

Q2:   Which one of the following is the entry level certification for an individual?
   A.  TOGAF 9 Certified
   B.  TOGAF 9 Foundation
   C.  TOGAF 9 Professional
   D.  TOGAF 9 Architect

6   Additional time is allowed for candidates for whom English is a second language where the examination is not available in the local language. For further information see the advice to candidates sheet on The Open Group TOGAF 9 Certification web site.

Q3:   Which one of the following describes three principles of the TOGAF 9
      People certification program?
      A.   Integrity, Scalability, Flexibility
      B.   Objectivity, Robustness, Simplicity
      C.   Openness, Fairness, Quality
      D.   Knowledge-based, Valuable, Simplicity
      E.   All of these

Q4:   Which of the following topic areas is not included in the TOGAF 9
      Foundation Syllabus?
      A.   Architecture Governance
      B.   Basic Concepts
      C.   Building Blocks
      D.   Guidelines for adapting the ADM: Iteration and Levels
      E.   Introduction to the ADM

Q5:   All of the following apply to the TOGAF 9 Part 1 Examination, except
      which statement?
      A.   Candidates who fail cannot take the examination again within one
           (1) month.
      B.   The examination consists of more than 100 questions.
      C.   The examination has multiple-choice format questions.
      D.   It is a closed-book examination.

## 1.5  Recommended Reading

The following are recommended sources of further information for this
chapter:
• TOGAF Certification for People: Program Summary Datasheet, February
  2009, published by The Open Group (www.opengroup.org/togaf9/cert/
  docs/togaf9_cert_summary.pdf)
• TOGAF 9 Foundation Datasheet, February 2009, published by The Open
  Group (www.opengroup.org/togaf9/cert/docs/togaf9_foundation.pdf)
• TOGAF Certification for People: Certification Policy, February 2009
  (X091), published by The Open Group (www.opengroup.org/bookstore/
  catalog/x091.htm)

- TOGAF Certification for People: Conformance Requirements (Multi-Level), to December 2011 (X111), published by The Open Group (www.opengroup.org/bookstore/catalog/x111.htm)
- The Open Group TOGAF 9 Certification web site: www.opengroup.org/togaf9/cert
- The TOGAF information web site: www.togaf.info

# Chapter 2

# Basic Concepts

## 2.1 Key Learning Points

This chapter will familiarize you with the fundamentals that you need to know to pass the TOGAF 9 Part 1 Examination. The objectives of this chapter are as follows:

- To provide an introduction to the basic concepts of enterprise architecture and TOGAF, including providing a high-level view of TOGAF, enterprise architecture, architecture frameworks, and the contents of TOGAF 9

**Key Points Explained**

This chapter will help you to answer the following questions:

- What is TOGAF?
- What is an enterprise?
- What is enterprise architecture?
- Why do I need enterprise architecture? What are the business benefits?
- What is "architecture" in the context of TOGAF?
- What is an architecture framework?
- Why do I need a framework for enterprise architecture?
- Why is TOGAF suitable as a framework for enterprise architecture?
- What does TOGAF contain?
- What are the different types of architecture that TOGAF deals with?

## 2.2 Introduction to TOGAF 9

### 2.2.1 What is TOGAF?

*(Syllabus Reference: Unit 1, Learning Outcome 7: You should be able to briefly explain what TOGAF is.)*

TOGAF is an architecture framework – The Open Group Architecture Framework. TOGAF is a tool for assisting in the acceptance, production, use, and maintenance of enterprise architectures. It is based on an iterative process model supported by best practices and a re-usable set of existing architectural assets.

TOGAF is developed and maintained by The Open Group Architecture Forum. The first version of TOGAF, developed in 1995, was based on the US Department of Defense Technical Architecture Framework for Information Management (TAFIM). Starting from this sound foundation, The Open Group Architecture Forum has developed successive versions of TOGAF at regular intervals and published each one on The Open Group public web site.

This document covers TOGAF Version 9.1, referred to as "TOGAF 9" within the text of this document. TOGAF 9.1 is a maintenance update and was published in December 2011. It supersedes the original TOGAF 9 that was published in January 2009.

TOGAF 9 can be used for developing a broad range of different enterprise architectures. TOGAF complements, and can be used in conjunction with, other frameworks that are more focused on specific deliverables for particular vertical sectors such as Government, Telecommunications, Manufacturing, Defense, and Finance. The key to TOGAF is the method – the TOGAF Architecture Development Method (ADM) – for developing an enterprise architecture that addresses business needs.

When appropriate, this Study Guide contains references to sections within TOGAF, which are referred to as "the TOGAF document". The references are intended to be functional for the web version and printed version of the document. Therefore, the format of the reference number contains both the Part and the Chapter reference, but not the page references since they exist only in the printed book.

### 2.2.2  Structure of the TOGAF Document
*(Syllabus Reference: Unit 1, Learning Outcome 6: You should be able to describe the structure of TOGAF, and briefly explain the contents of each of the parts.)*

Table 3 summarizes the parts of the TOGAF document.

Table 3: Structure of the TOGAF Document

| TOGAF Part | Summary |
| --- | --- |
| Part I: Introduction | This part provides a high-level introduction to the key concepts of enterprise architecture and, in particular, to the TOGAF approach. It contains the definitions of terms used throughout TOGAF and release notes detailing the changes between this version and the previous version of TOGAF. |
| Part II: Architecture Development Method (ADM) | This part is the core of TOGAF. It describes the TOGAF Architecture Development Method (ADM) – a step-by-step approach to developing an enterprise architecture. |
| Part III: ADM Guidelines and Techniques | This part contains a collection of guidelines and techniques available for use in applying the ADM. |
| Part IV: Architecture Content Framework | This part describes the TOGAF content framework, including a structured metamodel for architectural artifacts, the use of re-usable Architecture Building Blocks (ABBs), and an overview of typical architecture deliverables. |
| Part V: Enterprise Continuum and Tools | This part discusses appropriate taxonomies and tools to categorize and store the outputs of architecture activity within an enterprise. |
| Part VI: TOGAF Reference Models | This part provides two architectural reference models, namely the TOGAF Technical Reference Model (TRM), and the Integrated Information Infrastructure Reference Model (III-RM). |
| Part VII: Architecture Capability Framework | This part discusses the organization, processes, skills, roles, and responsibilities required to establish and operate an architecture practice within an enterprise. |

## 2.3 What is an Enterprise?

*(Syllabus Reference: Unit 1, Learning Outcome 1: You should be able describe what an enterprise is.)*

TOGAF defines an "enterprise" as any collection of organizations that has a common set of goals. For example, an enterprise could be a government agency, a whole corporation, a division of a corporation, a single department, or a chain of geographically distant organizations linked together by common ownership.

The term "enterprise" in the context of "enterprise architecture" can be used to denote both an entire enterprise, encompassing all of its information systems, and a specific domain within the enterprise. In both cases, the architecture crosses multiple systems and multiple functional groups within the enterprise.

> Confusion often arises from the evolving nature of the term "enterprise". An extended enterprise frequently includes partners, suppliers, and customers. If the goal is to integrate an extended enterprise, then the enterprise comprises the partners, suppliers, and customers, as well as internal business units.
> For example, an organization with an online store that uses an external fulfillment house for dispatching orders would extend its definition of the enterprise in that system to include the fulfillment house.

## 2.4  What is Architecture in the Context of TOGAF?

*(Syllabus Reference: Unit 1, Learning Outcome 8: You should be able to explain what architecture is in the context of TOGAF.)*

ISO/IEC 42010:2007[7] defines "architecture" as:

*"The fundamental organization of a system, embodied in its components, their relationships to each other and the environment, and the principles governing its design and evolution."*

TOGAF embraces but does not strictly adhere to ISO/IEC 42010:2007 terminology. In TOGAF, "architecture" has two meanings depending upon the context:

1.  A formal description of a system, or a detailed plan of the system at a component level to guide its implementation
2.  The structure of components, their inter-relationships, and the principles and guidelines governing their design and evolution over time

---

7    ISO/IEC 42010:2007, Systems and Software Engineering – Recommended Practice for Architectural Description of Software-Intensive Systems, Edition 1 (technically identical to ANSI/IEEE Std 1471-2000).

**What is enterprise architecture?**

There are many definitions of enterprise architecture. Most focus on structure and organization. Two definitions are given below:

**Enterprise architecture** is:

1. The organizing logic for business processes and IT infrastructure reflecting the integration and standardization requirements of the firm's operating model. [Source: MIT Center for Information Systems Research]

2. A conceptual blueprint that defines the structure and operation of an organization. The intent of an enterprise architecture is to determine how an organization can most effectively achieve its current and future objectives. [Source: SearchCIO.com]

## 2.5 Why do I Need Enterprise Architecture?

*(Syllabus Reference: Unit 1, Learning Outcome 2: You should be able to explain the purpose of an enterprise architecture.)*

The purpose of enterprise architecture is to optimize across the enterprise the often fragmented legacy of processes (both manual and automated) into an integrated environment that is responsive to change and supportive of the delivery of the business strategy. Effective management and exploitation of information through IT is a key factor to business success, and an indispensable means to achieving competitive advantage. An enterprise architecture addresses this need, by providing a strategic context for the evolution of the IT system in response to the constantly changing needs of the business environment.

*(Syllabus Reference: Unit 1, Learning Outcome 3: You should be able to list the business benefits of having an enterprise architecture.)*

The advantages that result from a good enterprise architecture can bring important business benefits, including:
- A more efficient business operation:
  — Lower business operation costs
  — More agile organization
  — Business capabilities shared across the organization

- — Lower change management costs
- — More flexible workforce
- — Improved business productivity
- A more efficient IT operation:
  - — Lower software development, support, and maintenance costs
  - — Increased portability of applications
  - — Improved interoperability and easier system and network management
  - — Improved ability to address critical enterprise-wide issues, such as security
  - — Easier upgrade and exchange of system components
- Better return on existing investment, reduced risk for future investment:
  - — Reduced complexity in the business and IT
  - — Maximum return on investment in existing business and IT infrastructure
  - — The flexibility to make, buy, or out-source business and IT solutions
  - — Reduced risk overall in new investments and their costs of ownership
- Faster, simpler, and cheaper procurement:
  - — Simpler buying decisions, because the information governing procurement is readily available in a coherent plan
  - — Faster procurement process, maximizing procurement speed and flexibility without sacrificing architectural coherence
  - — The ability to procure heterogeneous, multi-vendor open systems
  - — The ability to secure more economic capabilities

Ultimately, the benefits of enterprise architecture derive from the better planning, earlier visibility, and more informed designs that result when it is introduced.
[Source: Simon Townson, Why Does Enterprise Architecture Matter?]

## 2.6  What is an Architecture Framework?

*(Syllabus Reference: Unit 1, Learning Outcome 4: You should be able to define what an architecture framework is.)*

An architecture framework is a foundational structure, or set of structures, that can be used for developing a broad range of different architectures. It should describe a method for designing a target state of the enterprise in terms of a set of building blocks, and for showing how the building blocks fit together. It should contain a set of tools and provide a common vocabulary. It should also include a list of recommended standards and compliant products that can be used to implement the building blocks.

## 2.7  Why do I Need a Framework for Enterprise Architecture?

Using an architecture framework will speed up and simplify architecture development, ensure more complete coverage of the designed solution, and make certain that the architecture selected allows for future growth in response to the needs of the business.

**Regulatory Drivers for Adoption of Enterprise Architecture**

There are a number of laws and regulations that have been drivers for the adoption and use of enterprise architecture in business:

- The Clinger-Cohen Act

  (US Information Technology Management Reform Act 1996)

  The US Information Technology Management Reform Act (Clinger-Cohen Act) is designed to improve the way the US Federal Government acquires and manages IT. It mandates the use of a formal enterprise architecture process for all US federal agencies.

- The Sarbanes-Oxley Act

  (US Public Company Accounting Reform and Investor Protection Act 2002)

  The Sarbanes-Oxley Act was passed in response to a number of major corporate and accounting scandals involving prominent companies in the US (for example, Enron and Worldcom). Under the Act, companies must provide attestation of internal control assessment, including documentation of control procedures related to IT.

- EU Directives on the Award of Public Contracts

  Similarly within the European Union, there are EU Directives that require vendors involved in Public Contracts to show that they are using formal enterprise architecture processes within their businesses when supplying products and services.

## 2.8 Why is TOGAF Suitable as a Framework for Enterprise Architecture?

*(Syllabus Reference: Unit 1, Learning Outcome 5: You should be able explain why TOGAF is suitable as a framework for enterprise architecture.)*

TOGAF has been developed through the collaborative efforts of more than 300 Architecture Forum member companies from some of the world's leading companies and organizations. Using TOGAF results in enterprise architecture that is consistent, reflects the needs of stakeholders, employs best practice, and gives due consideration both to current requirements and to the perceived future needs of the business.

Developing and sustaining an enterprise architecture is a technically complex process which involves many stakeholders and decision processes in the organization. TOGAF plays an important role in standardizing and risk reduction of the architecture development process. TOGAF provides a best practice framework for adding value, and enables the organization to build workable and economic solutions which address their business issues and needs.

## 2.9 What are the Different Architecture Domains that TOGAF deals with?

*(Syllabus Reference: Unit 1, Learning Outcome 9: You should be able to list the different types of architecture that TOGAF deals with.)*

TOGAF 9 covers the development of four architecture domains. These are commonly accepted as subsets of an overall enterprise architecture, all of which TOGAF is designed to support. They are as follows:

Table 4:   Architecture Domains Supported by TOGAF

| Architecture Type | Description |
| --- | --- |
| Business Architecture | The business strategy, governance, organization, and key business processes. |
| Data Architecture | The structure of an organization's logical and physical data assets and data management resources. |
| Application Architecture | A blueprint for the individual application systems to be deployed, their interactions, and their relationships to the core business processes of the organization. |

| Architecture Type | Description |
|---|---|
| Technology Architecture | The software and hardware capabilities that are required to support the deployment of business, data, and application services. This includes IT infrastructure, middleware, networks, communications, processing, and standards. |

## 2.10 What does TOGAF Contain?

*(Syllabus Reference: Unit 1, Learning Outcome 6: You should be able to describe the structure of TOGAF, and briefly explain the contents of each part.)*

TOGAF reflects the structure and content of an architecture capability within an enterprise, as shown in Figure 4.

**Definition of "Capability"**

An ability that an organization, person, or system possesses. Capabilities are typically expressed in general and high-level terms and typically require a combination of organization, people, processes, and technology to achieve. For example, marketing, customer contact, or outbound telemarketing.
[Source: TOGAF 9 Part I: Introduction, Chapter 3 (Definitions)]

An **enterprise architecture capability** (or architecture capability) in the context of TOGAF, is the ability for an organization to effectively undertake the activities of an enterprise architecture practice.

Central to TOGAF is the Architecture Development Method (documented in TOGAF 9 Part II: ADM). The architecture capability (documented in TOGAF 9 Part VII: Architecture Capability Framework) operates the method. The method is supported by a number of guidelines and techniques (documented in TOGAF 9 Part III: ADM Guidelines and Techniques). This produces content to be stored in the repository (documented in TOGAF 9 Part IV: Architecture Content Framework), which is classified according to the Enterprise Continuum (documented in TOGAF 9 Part V: Enterprise Continuum and Tools). The repository is initially populated with the TOGAF Reference Models (documented in TOGAF 9 Part VI: TOGAF Reference Models).

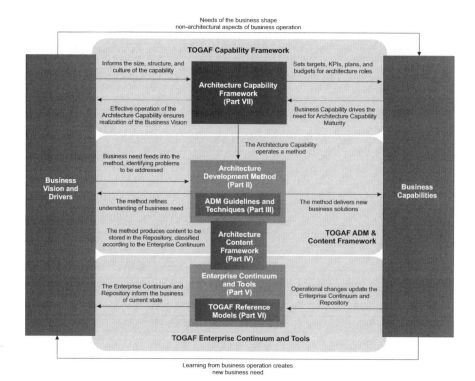

Figure 4:   TOGAF Content Overview

These are described in the following sections.

## 2.10.1  The Architecture Development Method (ADM)

The ADM describes a process for deriving an organization-specific enterprise
architecture that addresses business requirements.

The ADM is the major component of TOGAF and provides guidance for
architects on a number of levels:

- It provides a number of **architecture development phases** (Business
  Architecture, Information Systems Architectures, Technology
  Architecture) in a cycle, as an overall process template for architecture
  development activity.

- It provides a **narrative of each architecture phase**, describing the phase
  in terms of objectives, approach, inputs, steps, and outputs. The inputs
  and outputs sections provide a definition of the architecture content
  structure and deliverables (a detailed description of the phase inputs and
  phase outputs is given in the Architecture Content Framework).

- It provides cross-phase summaries that cover requirements management.

See also Chapter 5 and Chapter 7.

### 2.10.2 ADM Guidelines and Techniques

**ADM Guidelines and Techniques** provides a number of guidelines and techniques to support the application of the ADM. The guidelines address adapting the ADM to deal with a number of usage scenarios, including different process styles (e.g., the use of iteration) and also specific specialty architectures (such as security). The techniques support specific tasks within the ADM (such as defining principles, business scenarios, gap analysis, migration planning, risk management, etc.).

See also Chapter 8.

### 2.10.3 Architecture Content Framework

The **Architecture Content Framework** provides a detailed model of architectural work products, including deliverables, artifacts within deliverables, and the Architecture Building Blocks (ABBs) that deliverables represent.

The details of the Architecture Content Framework are out of scope for TOGAF 9 Foundation, and are covered instead in the Level 2 syllabus.

### 2.10.4 The Enterprise Continuum

The **Enterprise Continuum** provides a model for structuring a virtual repository and provides methods for classifying architecture and solution artifacts, showing how the different types of artifacts evolve, and how they can be leveraged and re-used. This is based on architectures and solutions (models, patterns, architecture descriptions, etc.) that exist within the enterprise and in the industry at large, and which the enterprise has collected for use in the development of its architectures.

See also Section 3.4 and Chapter 6.

### 2.10.5 TOGAF Reference Models

TOGAF provides two reference models for possible inclusion in an enterprise's own Enterprise Continuum.

Table 5:    Reference Models Included in the Enterprise Continuum

| Reference Model | Description |
|---|---|
| TOGAF Foundation Architecture Technical Reference Model | The TOGAF Technical Reference Model is an architecture of generic services and functions that provides a foundation on which specific architectures and Architecture Building Blocks (ABBs) can be built. |
| Integrated Information Infrastructure Reference Model (III-RM) | The Integrated Information Infrastructure Reference Model (III-RM) is based on the TOGAF Foundation Architecture, and is specifically aimed at helping the design of architectures that enable and support the vision of Boundaryless Information Flow. |

See also Chapter 13.

### 2.10.6  The Architecture Capability Framework

The **Architecture Capability Framework** is a set of resources, guidelines, templates, background information, etc. provided to help the architect establish an architecture practice within an organization.

See also Section 3.6, Section 3.7, and Chapter 9.

## 2.11  Summary

This chapter has introduced the basic concepts of enterprise architecture and TOGAF. This has included answering questions, such as:

- "What is an enterprise?"
    - A collection of organizations that share a common set of goals, such as a government agency, part of a corporation, or a corporation in its entirety.
    - Large corporations may comprise multiple enterprises.
    - An "extended enterprise" can include partners, suppliers, and customers.
- "What is an architecture?"
    - An architecture is defined as "the fundamental organization of something, embodied in its components, their relationships to each other and the environment, and the principles governing its design and evolution."

TOGAF is an architecture framework. It enables you to design, evaluate, and build the right architecture for your organization. An architecture framework is a toolkit that can be used for developing a broad range of different architectures.

- It should describe a method to design an information system in terms of a set of building blocks, and show how the building blocks fit together.
- It should contain a set of tools and provide a common vocabulary.
- It should also include a list of recommended standards and compliant products that can be used to implement the building blocks.

The value of a framework is that it provides a practical starting point for an architecture project.

The components of TOGAF 9 are as follows:
- Architecture Development Method (ADM)
- ADM Guidelines and Techniques
- The Architecture Content Framework
- The Enterprise Continuum and Tools
- TOGAF Reference Models
- The Architecture Capability Framework

## 2.12  Test Yourself Questions

Q1:   Which one of the following statements best describes TOGAF?
- A.   TOGAF is a tool for developing Technology Architectures only.
- B.   TOGAF is a framework and method for architecture development.
- C.   TOGAF is a business model.
- D.   TOGAF is a specific architecture pattern.
- E.   TOGAF is a method for IT Governance

Q2:   Which one of the following best describes why you need a framework for enterprise architecture?
- A.   Architecture design is complex.
- B.   Using a framework can speed up the process.
- C.   Using a framework ensures more complete coverage.
- D.   A framework provides a set of tools and a common vocabulary.
- E.   All of these.

Q3: Which of the following is *not* considered one of the main constituent parts of the TOGAF document?
  A. The Architecture Development Method
  B. The Enterprise Continuum & Tools
  C. The Technical Reference Model
  D. The TOGAF Architecture Capability Framework

Q4: Which one of the types of architecture below is *not* commonly accepted as part of the enterprise architecture addressed by TOGAF?
  A. Business Architecture
  B. Data Architecture
  C. Application Architecture
  D. Technology Architecture
  E. Pattern Architecture

Q5: Which part of the TOGAF document provides a number of architecture development phases, together with narratives for each phase?
  A. Part I: Introduction
  B. Part II: Architecture Development Method (ADM)
  C. Part III: ADM Guidelines and Techniques
  D. Part IV: Architecture Content Framework
  E. Part V: Enterprise Continuum and Tools

## 2.13  Recommended Reading

The following are recommended sources of further information for this chapter:

- TOGAF 9 Part I: Introduction, Chapter 1 (Introduction) and Chapter 2 (Core Concepts).
- Why Does Enterprise Architecture Matter?, White Paper by Simon Townson, SAP, November 2008 (W076), published by The Open Group (www.opengroup.org/bookstore/catalog/w076.htm)

Chapter 3

# Core Concepts

## 3.1 Key Learning Points

This chapter will help you understand and be able to explain the core concepts of TOGAF.

**Key Points Explained**

This chapter will help you to answer the following questions:

- What are the ADM phase names and the purpose of each phase?
- What are deliverables, artifacts, and building blocks?
- What is the Enterprise Continuum?
- What is the Architecture Repository?
- How to establish and operate an enterprise architecture capability?
- How to use TOGAF with other frameworks?

## 3.2 What are the Phases of the ADM?

*(Syllabus Reference: Unit 2, Learning Outcome 1: You should be able to explain the core concept of the ADM and the purpose of each phase at a high level.)*

The Architecture Development Method (ADM) forms the core of TOGAF and is a method for deriving organization-specific enterprise architecture. It is the result of contributions from many architecture practitioners.

The ADM provides a tested and repeatable process for developing architectures. The ADM includes establishing an architecture framework, developing architecture content, transitioning, and governing the realization of architectures. All of these activities are carried out within an iterative cycle of continuous architecture definition and realization that allows organizations to transform their enterprises in a controlled manner in response to business goals and opportunities.

The ADM is described as a number of phases within a process of change illustrated by an ADM cycle graphic (see following). Phases within the ADM are as follows:

The **Preliminary Phase** describes the preparation and initiation activities required to create an Architecture Capability, including the customization of TOGAF, and the definition of Architecture Principles.

**Phase A: Architecture Vision** describes the initial phase of an Architecture Development Cycle. It includes information about defining the scope, identifying the stakeholders, creating the Architecture Vision, and obtaining approvals.

**Phase B: Business Architecture** describes the development of a Business Architecture to support an agreed Architecture Vision.

**Phase C: Information Systems Architectures** describes the development of Information Systems Architectures for an architecture project, including the development of Data and Application Architectures.

**Phase D: Technology Architecture** describes the development of the Technology Architecture for an architecture project.

**Phase E: Opportunities and Solutions** describes the process of identifying major implementation projects and grouping them into work packages that deliver the Target Architecture defined in the previous phases.

**Phase F: Migration Planning** describes the development of a detailed Implementation and Migration Plan that addresses how to move from the Baseline to the Target Architecture.

**Phase G: Implementation Governance** provides an architectural oversight of the implementation.

**Phase H: Architecture Change Management** establishes procedures for managing change to the new architecture.

**Requirements Management** examines the process of managing architecture requirements throughout the ADM.

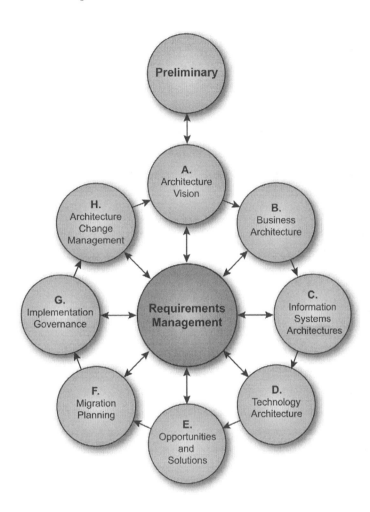

## 3.3 Deliverables, Artifacts, and Building Blocks

*(Syllabus Reference: Unit 2, Learning Outcome 2: You should be able to explain the core concepts of deliverables, artifacts, and building blocks in the context of the Architecture Content Framework.)*

During application of the ADM process, a number of outputs are produced; for example, process flows, architectural requirements, project plans, project compliance assessments, etc. In order to collate and present these major work products in a consistent and structured manner, TOGAF defines a structural model – the TOGAF Architecture Content Framework – in which to place them.

The Architecture Content Framework uses the following three categories to describe the type of architectural work product within the context of use:

- A **deliverable** is a work product that is contractually specified and in turn formally reviewed, agreed, and signed off by the stakeholders. Deliverables represent the output of projects and those deliverables that are in documentation form will typically be archived at completion of a project, or transitioned into an Architecture Repository as a reference model, standard, or snapshot of the Architecture Landscape at a point in time.
- An **artifact** is an architectural work product that describes an aspect of the architecture. Artifacts are generally classified as catalogs (lists of things), matrices (showing relationships between things), and diagrams (pictures of things). Examples include a requirements catalog, business interaction matrix, and a use-case diagram. An architectural deliverable may contain many artifacts and artifacts will form the content of the Architecture Repository.
- A **building block** represents a (potentially re-usable) component of business, IT, or architectural capability that can be combined with other building blocks to deliver architectures and solutions.

Building blocks can be defined at various levels of detail and can relate to both architectures and solutions, with Architecture Building Blocks (ABBs) typically describing the required capability in order to shape the Solution Building Blocks (SBBs) which would represent the components to be used to implement the required capability.

The relationships between deliverables, artifacts, and building blocks are shown in Figure 5.

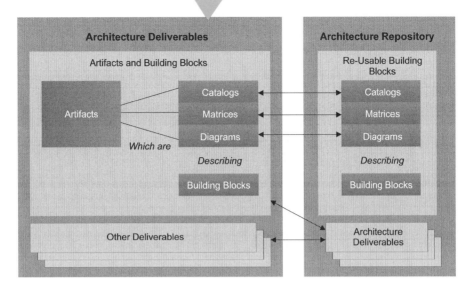

Figure 5:    Relationships between Deliverables, Artifacts, and Building Blocks

## 3.4  The Enterprise Continuum

*(Syllabus Reference: Unit 2, Learning Outcome 3: You should be able to explain the core concept of the Enterprise Continuum.)*

TOGAF includes the concept of the Enterprise Continuum, shown in Figure 6, which sets the broader context for an architect and explains how generic solutions can be leveraged and specialized in order to support the requirements of an individual organization. The Enterprise Continuum is a view of the Architecture Repository that provides methods for classifying architecture and solution artifacts as they evolve from generic Foundation Architectures to Organization-Specific Architectures. The Enterprise Continuum comprises two complementary concepts: the Architecture Continuum and the Solutions Continuum.

**The Enterprise Continuum and the Architecture Repository**

The Enterprise Continuum provides a view of the Architecture Repository that shows the evolution of these related architectures from generic to specific, from abstract to concrete, and from logical to physical.

[Source: TOGAF 9 Part V: Enterprise Continuum and Tools]

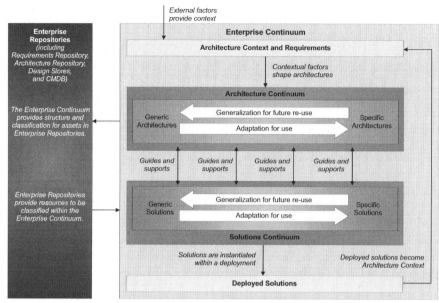

Figure 6:    The Enterprise Continuum

## 3.5  **The Architecture Repository**

*(Syllabus Reference: Unit 2, Learning Outcome 4: You should be able to explain the core concept of the Architecture Repository.)*

Supporting the Enterprise Continuum is the concept of an Architecture Repository which can be used to store different classes of architectural output at different levels of abstraction, created by the ADM. In this way, TOGAF facilitates understanding and co-operation between stakeholders and practitioners at different levels.

The structure of the TOGAF Architecture Repository is shown in Figure 7.

The major components within an Architecture Repository are as follows:
*   The **Architecture Metamodel** describes the organizationally tailored application of an architecture framework, including a metamodel for architecture content.
*   The **Architecture Capability** defines the parameters, structures, and processes that support governance of the Architecture Repository.
*   The **Architecture Landscape** shows an architectural view of the building blocks that are in use within the organization today (e.g., a list of the

live applications). The landscape is likely to exist at multiple levels of abstraction to suit different architecture objectives.

- The **Standards Information Base (SIB)**[8] captures the standards with which new architectures must comply, which may include industry standards, selected products and services from suppliers, or shared services already deployed within the organization.
- The **Reference Library** provides guidelines, templates, patterns, and other forms of reference material that can be leveraged in order to accelerate the creation of new architectures for the enterprise.
- The **Governance Log** provides a record of governance activity across the enterprise.

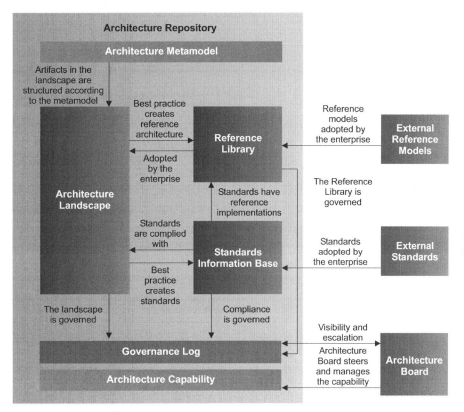

Figure 7:   TOGAF Architecture Repository Structure

---

8    An example SIB can be found on The Open Group website at www.opengroup.org/sib.

## 3.6 Establishing and Maintaining an Enterprise Architecture Capability

*(Syllabus Reference: Unit 2, Learning Outcome 5: You should be able to explain the core concept of establishing and maintaining an Enterprise Architecture Capability.)*

TOGAF 9 provides an Architecture Capability Framework that is a set of reference materials and guidelines for establishing an architecture function or capability within an organization. A summary of the contents is shown in Table 6.

Table 6:   Architecture Capability Framework Contents Summary

| Chapter | Description |
|---|---|
| Establishing an Architecture Capability | Guidelines for establishing an Architecture Capability within an organization. |
| Architecture Board | Guidelines for establishing and operating an enterprise Architecture Board. |
| Architecture Compliance | Guidelines for ensuring project compliance to architecture. |
| Architecture Contracts | Guidelines for defining and using Architecture Contracts. |
| Architecture Governance | Framework and guidelines for Architecture Governance. |
| Architecture Maturity Models | Techniques for evaluating and quantifying an organization's maturity in enterprise architecture. |
| Architecture Skills Framework | A set of role, skill, and experience norms for staff undertaking enterprise architecture work. |

An overall structure for an Architecture Capability Framework is shown in Figure 8.

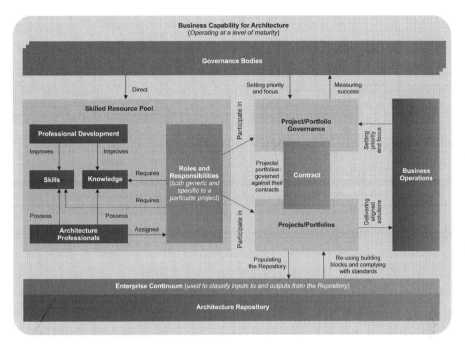

Figure 8:   Architecture Capability Framework

## 3.7 Establishing an Operational Architecture Capability

*(Syllabus Reference: Unit 2, Learning Outcome 6: You should be able to explain the core concept of establishing the Architecture Capability as an operational entity.)*

An enterprise architecture practice must be run like any other operational unit within a business; i.e., it should be treated like a business. To this end, and over and above the core processes defined within the ADM, an enterprise architecture practice should establish capabilities in the following areas:

- Financial Management
- Performance Management
- Service Management
- Risk Management
- Resource Management
- Communications and Stakeholder Management
- Quality Management
- Supplier Management
- Configuration Management
- Environment Management

Central to the notion of operating an ongoing architecture is the execution of well-defined and effective governance – Architecture Governance – whereby all architecturally significant activity is controlled and aligned within a single framework.

The benefits of Architecture Governance include:

- Increased transparency of accountability, and informed delegation of authority
- Controlled risk management
- Protection of the existing asset base through maximizing re-use of existing architectural components
- Proactive control, monitoring, and management mechanisms
- Process, concept, and component re-use across all organizational business units
- Value creation through monitoring, measuring, evaluation, and feedback
- Increased visibility supporting internal processes and external parties' requirements; in particular, increased visibility of decision-making at lower levels ensures oversight at an appropriate level within the enterprise of decisions that may have far-reaching strategic consequences for the organization
- Greater shareholder value; in particular, enterprise architecture increasingly represents the core intellectual property of the enterprise – studies have demonstrated a correlation between increased shareholder value and well-governed enterprises
- Integrates with existing processes and methodologies and complements functionality by adding control capabilities

## 3.8  Using TOGAF with Other Frameworks

*(Syllabus Reference: Unit 2, Learning Outcome 7: You should be able to explain the core concept of the use of TOGAF with other frameworks.)*

Two of the key elements of any enterprise architecture framework are a definition of the deliverables that the architecting activity should produce, together with a description of the method for production.

Many enterprise architecture frameworks focus on the first of these – the specific set of deliverables – and are relatively silent about the methods to be used to generate them.

Because TOGAF is a generic framework and intended to be used in a wide variety of environments, it provides a flexible and extensible content framework that underpins a set of generic architecture deliverables. As a result, TOGAF may be used either in its own right, with the generic deliverables that it describes; or else these deliverables may be replaced or extended by a more specific set, defined in any other framework that the architect considers relevant.

In all cases, it is expected that the architect will adapt and build on the TOGAF framework in order to define a tailored method that is integrated into the processes and organization structures of the enterprise. This architecture tailoring may include adopting elements from other architecture frameworks, or integrating TOGAF methods with other standard frameworks, such as ITIL, CMMI, COBIT, PRINCE2, PMBOK, and MSP.

As a generic framework and method for enterprise architecture, TOGAF also complements other frameworks that are aimed at specific vertical business domains, specific horizontal technology areas (such as security or manageability), or specific application areas (such as e-Commerce).

**Key Fact**

Why is TOGAF becoming so popular in the industry?

One key reason is that architects can use the TOGAF ADM in conjunction with any of the popular frameworks.

The TOGAF ADM is framework-agnostic, and helps IT architects fill in the framework they might already have in use.

[Source: Bill Estrem, "TOGAF to the Rescue" (www.opengroup.org/downloads)]

## 3.9  Summary

This chapter has introduced the core concepts of TOGAF. This has included the following:

- The ADM and the purpose of each phase
- The concepts of deliverables, artifacts, and building blocks, and how they relate to the outputs of the ADM
- The Enterprise Continuum as a concept, and how it is used to classify artifacts

- The Architecture Repository and how it is used to store different classes of architectural output
- How to establish and maintain an enterprise architecture capability, and the guidelines available within TOGAF
- How to operate an architecture capability, including a list of recommended capabilities beyond the ADM
- The use of TOGAF with other frameworks, and how TOGAF may be used on its own or in conjunction with another framework

## 3.10  Test Yourself Questions

Q1:    Which of the TOGAF Architecture Development phases is the initial phase of an Architecture Development Cycle?
A.   Preliminary Phase
B.   Phase A
C.   Phase B
D.   Phase C
E.   Phase D

Q2:    Which of the TOGAF Architecture Development phases provides oversight of the implementation?
A.   Phase D
B.   Phase E
C.   Phase F
D.   Phase G
E.   Phase H

Q3.    Which of the TOGAF Architecture Development phases includes the creation and approval of the Architecture Vision document?
A.   Preliminary Phase
B.   Phase A
C.   Phase B
D.   Phase C
E.   Phase D

Q4. Which of the following is *not* a phase of the ADM?
    A. Preliminary
    B. Phase C: Requirements Architecture
    C. Phase F: Migration Planning
    D. Phase D: Technology Architecture
    E. Phase G: Implementation Governance

Q5: Which of the following is defined as a work product that describes an aspect of an architecture?
    A. An artifact
    B. A building block
    C. A catalog
    D. A deliverable
    E. A matrix

Q6: Complete the sentence: The Enterprise Continuum is _____
    A. An architecture framework
    B. A database of open industry standards
    C. A technical reference model
    D. A model for classifying artifacts
    E. A method for developing architectures

Q7: Which component of the Architecture Repository provides guidelines, templates, and patterns that can be used to create new architectures?
    A. The Architecture Metamodel
    B. The Architecture Capability
    C. The Architecture Landscape
    D. The Reference Library
    E. The Governance Log

## 3.11 Recommended Reading

The following are recommended sources of further information for this chapter:

- TOGAF 9 Part I: Introduction, Chapter 2 (Core Concepts)

Chapter 4

# Key Terminology

## 4.1 Key Learning Points

This chapter will help you understand the key terminology of TOGAF.

**Key Points Explained**

This chapter will help you to answer the following questions:

- What are the key terms for TOGAF 9 Foundation?
- Where are these terms used within this Study Guide?

The key terms listed and defined here are used in the rest of this Study Guide. The TOGAF 9 Foundation Syllabus expects candidates to be able to understand and explain the definitions marked as learning outcomes in this section, although notes that they are expected to be covered as part of the learning in other units. Please refer to this chapter when a term is used in other chapters and you need more information on its meaning.

## 4.2 Key Terms

*(Syllabus Reference: Unit 3, Learning Outcomes 1-45: You should understand and be able to explain the following defined terms from TOGAF.)*

**Application**
*(Syllabus Reference: Unit 3, Learning Outcome 1)*

A deployed and operational IT system that supports business functions and services; for example, a payroll. Applications use data and are supported by multiple technology components but are distinct from the technology components that support the application.

### Application Architecture
*(Syllabus Reference: Unit 3, Learning Outcome 2)*

A description of the major logical grouping of capabilities that manage the data objects necessary to process the data and support the business.

### Architecture
*(Syllabus Reference: Unit 3, Learning Outcome 3)*

Architecture has two meanings depending upon its contextual usage:
1.  A formal description of a system, or a detailed plan of the system at component level to guide its implementation
2.  The structure of components, their inter-relationships, and the principles and guidelines governing their design and evolution over time

See also Chapter 2.

### Architecture Continuum
A part of the Enterprise Continuum. A repository of architectural elements with increasing detail and specialization. This Continuum begins with foundational definitions such as reference models, core strategies, and basic building blocks. From there it spans to Industry Architectures and all the way to an organization's specific architecture.

See also Chapter 6.

### Architecture Building Block (ABB)
*(Syllabus Reference: Unit 3, Learning Outcome 4)*

A constituent of the architecture model that describes a single aspect of the overall model.

See also Building Block and Chapter 11.

### Architecture Development Method (ADM)
*(Syllabus Reference: Unit 3, Learning Outcome 5)*

The core of TOGAF. A step-by-step approach to develop and use an enterprise architecture.

See also Chapter 2, Chapter 5, and Chapter 7.

**Architecture Domain**
*(Syllabus Reference: Unit 3, Learning Outcome 6)*

The architectural area being considered. There are four architecture domains within TOGAF: Business, Data, Application, and Technology.

> **BDAT (Business – Data – Application – Technology)**
> A simple mnemonic to aid remembering the four architecture domains.

**Architecture Framework**
*(Syllabus Reference: Unit 3, Learning Outcome 7)*

A conceptual structure used to develop, implement, and sustain an architecture.

See also Chapter 2.

**Architecture Principles**
*(Syllabus Reference: Unit 3, Learning Outcome 8)*

A qualitative statement of intent that should be met by the architecture. Has at least a supporting rationale and a measure of importance.

See also Chapter 8.

**Architecture Vision**
*(Syllabus Reference: Unit 3, Learning Outcome 9)*

A succinct description of the Target Architecture that describes its business value and the changes to the enterprise that will result from its successful deployment. It serves as an aspirational vision and a boundary for detailed architecture development.

See also Chapter 7 and Chapter 12.

**Baseline**
*(Syllabus Reference: Unit 3, Learning Outcome 10)*

A specification that has been formally reviewed and agreed upon, that thereafter serves as the basis for further development or change and that can be changed only through formal change control procedures or a type of procedure such as configuration management.

**Building Block**
*(Syllabus Reference: Unit 3, Learning Outcome 11)*

Represents a (potentially re-usable) component of business, IT, or architectural capability that can be combined with other building blocks to deliver architectures and solutions.

Building blocks can be defined at various levels of detail, depending on what stage of architecture development has been reached. For instance, at an early stage, a building block can simply consist of a name or an outline description. Later on, a building block may be decomposed into multiple supporting building blocks and may be accompanied by a full specification. Building blocks can relate to "architectures" or "solutions".

See also Section 3.3 and Chapter 11.

**Business Architecture**
*(Syllabus Reference: Unit 3, Learning Outcome 12)*

A description of the structure and interaction between the business strategy, organization, functions, business processes, and information needs.

See also Chapter 7.

**Business Governance**
*(Syllabus Reference: Unit 3, Learning Outcome 13)*

Concerned with ensuring that the business processes and policies (and their operation) deliver the business outcomes and adhere to relevant business regulation.

**Capability**
*(Syllabus Reference: Unit 3, Learning Outcome 14)*

An ability that an organization, person, or system possesses. Capabilities are typically expressed in general and high-level terms and typically require a combination of organization, people, processes, and technology to achieve; or example, marketing, customer contact, or outbound telemarketing.

**Concerns**
*(Syllabus Reference: Unit 3, Learning Outcome 15)*

The key interests that are crucially important to the stakeholders in a system, and determine the acceptability of the system. Concerns may pertain to any aspect of the system's functioning, development, or operation, including considerations such as performance, reliability, security, distribution, and evolvability.

See also Stakeholder and Chapter 10.

**Constraint**
*(Syllabus Reference: Unit 3, Learning Outcome 16)*

An external factor that prevents an organization from pursuing particular approaches to meet its goals; for example, customer data is not harmonized within the organization, regionally or nationally, constraining the organization's ability to offer effective customer service.

**Data Architecture**
*(Syllabus Reference: Unit 3, Learning Outcome 17)*

A description of the structure and interaction of the enterprise's major types and sources of data, logical data assets, physical data assets, and data management resources.

See also Chapter 7.

**Deliverable**
*(Syllabus Reference: Unit 3, Learning Outcome 18)*

An architectural work product that is contractually specified and in turn formally reviewed, agreed, and signed off by the stakeholders. Deliverables represent the output of projects and those deliverables that are in documentation form will typically be archived at completion of a project, or transitioned into an Architecture Repository as a reference model, standard, or snapshot of the Architecture Landscape at a point in time.

See also Chapter 2 and Chapter 12.

### Enterprise
*(Syllabus Reference: Unit 3, Learning Outcome 19)*

The highest level (typically) of description of an organization and typically covers all missions and functions. An enterprise will often span multiple organizations.

### Enterprise Continuum
A categorization mechanism useful for classifying architecture and solution artifacts, both internal and external to the Architecture Repository, as they evolve from generic Foundation Architectures to Organization-Specific Architectures.

See also Chapter 6.

### Foundation Architecture
*(Syllabus Reference: Unit 3, Learning Outcome 20)*

Generic building blocks, their inter-relationships with other building blocks, combined with the principles and guidelines that provide a foundation on which more specific architectures can be built.

See also Chapter 13.

### Gap
*(Syllabus Reference: Unit 3, Learning Outcome 21)*

A statement of difference between two states. Used in the context of gap analysis, where the difference between the Baseline and Target Architecture is identified.

See also Chapter 8.

### Governance
*(Syllabus Reference: Unit 3, Learning Outcome 22)*

The discipline of monitoring, managing, and steering a business (or IS/IT landscape) to deliver the business outcome required.

See also Chapter 9.

### Information
*(Syllabus Reference: Unit 3, Learning Outcome 23)*

Any communication or representation of facts, data, or opinions, in any medium or form, including textual, numerical, graphic, cartographic, narrative, or audio-visual.

### Information Technology (IT)
*(Syllabus Reference: Unit 3, Learning Outcome 24)*

1. The lifecycle management of information and related technology used by an organization.
2. An umbrella term that includes all or some of the subject areas relating to the computer industry, such as Business Continuity, Business IT Interface, Business Process Modeling and Management, Communication, Compliance and Legislation, Computers, Content Management, Hardware, Information Management, Internet, Offshoring, Networking, Programming and Software, Professional Issues, Project Management, Security, Standards, Storage, Voice and Data Communications. Various countries and industries employ other umbrella terms to describe this same collection.
3. A term commonly assigned to a department within an organization tasked with provisioning some or all of the domains described in (2) above.
4. Alternate names commonly adopted include Information Services, Information Management, etc.

### Logical (Architecture)
*(Syllabus Reference: Unit 3, Learning Outcome 25)*

An implementation-independent definition of the architecture, often grouping related physical entities according to their purpose and structure; for example, the products from multiple infrastructure software vendors can all be logically grouped as Java application server platforms.

### Metadata
*(Syllabus Reference: Unit 3, Learning Outcome 26)*

Data about data, of any sort in any media, that describes the characteristics of an entity.

### Metamodel
*(Syllabus Reference: Unit 3, Learning Outcome 27)*

A model that describes how and with what the architecture will be described in a structured way.

### Method
*(Syllabus Reference: Unit 3, Learning Outcome 28)*

A defined, repeatable approach to address a particular type of problem. See also Methodology.

### Methodology
*(Syllabus Reference: Unit 3, Learning Outcome 29)*

A defined, repeatable series of steps to address a particular type of problem, which typically centers on a defined process, but may also include definition of content.

See also Method.

### Model
*(Syllabus Reference: Unit 3, Learning Outcome 30)*

A representation of a subject of interest. A model provides a smaller scale, simplified, and/or abstract representation of the subject matter. A model is constructed as a "means to an end". In the context of enterprise architecture, the subject matter is a whole or part of the enterprise and the end is the ability to construct "views" that address the concerns of particular stakeholders; i.e., their "viewpoints" in relation to the subject matter.

See also Stakeholder, View, and Viewpoint.

### Modeling
*(Syllabus Reference: Unit 3, Learning Outcome 31)*

A technique through construction of models which enables a subject to be represented in a form that enables reasoning, insight, and clarity concerning the essence of the subject matter.

### Objective
*(Syllabus Reference: Unit 3, Learning Outcome 32)*

A time-bounded milestone for an organization used to demonstrate progress towards a goal; for example, "Increase Capacity Utilization by 30% by the end of 2009 to support the planned increase in market share".

### Physical
*(Syllabus Reference: Unit 3, Learning Outcome 33)*

A description of a real-world entity. Physical elements in an enterprise architecture may still be considerably abstracted from Solution Architecture, design, or implementation views.

### Reference Model (RM)
*(Syllabus Reference: Unit 3, Learning Outcome 34)*

A reference model is an abstract framework for understanding significant relationships among the entities of [an] environment, and for the development of consistent standards or specifications supporting that environment. A reference model is based on a small number of unifying concepts and may be used as a basis for education and explaining standards to a non-specialist. A reference model is not directly tied to any standards, technologies, or other concrete implementation details, but it does seek to provide common semantics that can be used unambiguously across and between different implementations.

See also Chapter 13.

### Repository
*(Syllabus Reference: Unit 3, Learning Outcome 35)*

A system that manages all of the data of an enterprise, including data and process models and other enterprise information. Hence, the data in a repository is much more extensive than that in a data dictionary, which generally defines only the data making up a database.

### Requirement
*(Syllabus Reference: Unit 3, Learning Outcome 36)*

A statement of need that must be met by a particular architecture or work package.

### Segment Architecture
A detailed, formal description of areas within an enterprise, used at the program or portfolio level to organize and align change activity.

### Solution Architecture
*(Syllabus Reference: Unit 3, Learning Outcome 37)*

A description of a discrete and focused business operation or activity and how IS/IT supports that operation. A Solution Architecture typically applies to a single project or project release, assisting in the translation of requirements into a solution vision, high-level business and/or IT system specifications, and a portfolio of implementation tasks.

### Solution Building Block
*(Syllabus Reference: Unit 3, Learning Outcome 38)*

A candidate solution which conforms to an Architecture Building Block (ABB).

See also Chapter 11.

**Solutions Continuum**
A part of the Enterprise Continuum. A repository of re-usable solutions for future implementation efforts. It contains implementations of the corresponding definitions in the Architecture Continuum.

See also Chapter 6.

**Stakeholder**
*(Syllabus Reference: Unit 3, Learning Outcome 39)*

An individual, team, or organization (or classes thereof) with interests in, or concerns relative to, the outcome of the architecture. Different stakeholders with different roles will have different concerns.

See also Chapter 10.

**Strategic Architecture**
*(Syllabus Reference: Unit 3, Learning Outcome 40)*

A summary formal description of the enterprise, providing an organizing framework for operational and change activity, and an executive-level, long-term view for direction setting.

**Target Architecture**
*(Syllabus Reference: Unit 3, Learning Outcome 41)*

The description of a future state of the architecture being developed for an organization. There may be several future states developed as a roadmap to show the evolution of the architecture to a target state.

**Technical Reference Model (TRM)**
A structure which allows the components of an information system to be described in a consistent manner.

See also Chapter 13.

### Technology Architecture

*(Syllabus Reference: Unit 3, Learning Outcome 42)*

A description of the structure and interaction of the platform services, and logical and physical technology components.

See also Chapter 7.

### Transition Architecture
*(Syllabus Reference: Unit 3, Learning Outcome 43)*

A formal description of one state of the architecture at an architecturally significant point in time. One or more Transition Architectures may be used to describe the progression in time from the Baseline to the Target Architecture.

### View
*(Syllabus Reference: Unit 3, Learning Outcome 44)*

The representation of a related set of concerns. A view is what is seen from a viewpoint. An architecture view may be represented by a model to demonstrate to stakeholders their areas of interest in the architecture. A view does not have to be visual or graphical in nature.

See also Chapter 10.

### Viewpoint
*(Syllabus Reference: Unit 3, Learning Outcome 45)*

A definition of the perspective from which a view is taken. It is a specification of the conventions for constructing and using a view (often by means of an appropriate schema or template). A view is what you see; a viewpoint is where you are looking from – the vantage point or perspective that determines what you see.

See also Chapter 10.

## 4.3  Summary

This chapter lists and defines the key terms used in this Study Guide and the TOGAF 9 Foundation Syllabus. These terms are used as part of the learning outcomes within other chapters of this Study Guide.

## 4.4  Test Yourself Questions

Q1:   Which one of the following is an architecture of generic services and functions?

A.   Application Architecture

B.   Foundation Architecture

C.   Segment Architecture

D.   Solution Architecture

Q2:   Which one of the following describes a statement of difference between two states?

A.   Baseline

B.   Constraint

C.   Deliverable

D.   Gap

E.   Viewpoint

Q3:   Which one of the following is defined as a categorization model for classifying architecture and solutions artifacts?

A.   Architecture Principle

B.   Architecture Repository

C.   Enterprise Continuum

D.   Foundation Architecture

Q4:   Which one of the following best defines an entity with interests in, or concerns relative to, the outcome of an architecture?

A.   Architect

B.   Sponsor

C.   Stakeholder

Q5:   Which one of the following is defined as formal description of the
      enterprise, providing an executive-level long-term view for direction
      setting?
      A.   Baseline Architecture
      B.   Business Architecture
      C.   Foundation Architecture
      D.   Segment Architecture
      E.   Strategic Architecture

Q6:   Which one of the following is defined as describing the state of an
      architecture at an architecturally significant point in time during the
      progression from the Baseline to the Target Architecture?
      A.   Capability Architecture
      B.   Foundation Architecture
      C.   Segment Architecture
      D.   Solution Architecture
      E.   Transition Architecture

## 4.5  Recommended Reading

The following are recommended sources of further information for this
chapter:

• TOGAF 9 Part I: Introduction, Chapter 3 (Definitions)

# Chapter 5

# Introduction to the Architecture Development Method

## 5.1 Key Learning Points

This chapter describes the Architecture Development Method (ADM) cycle, what it consists of, its relationship to the rest of TOGAF, and how to adapt and scope the ADM for use.

**Key Points Explained**

This chapter will help you to answer the following questions:

- What is the ADM cycle?
- What are the typical sets of steps within a phase?
- What is the versioning convention used for deliverables?
- What is its relationship to other parts of TOGAF?
- What is the purpose of the supporting guidelines and techniques?
- What is the difference between guidelines and techniques?
- What are the key points of the ADM cycle?
- Why would I need to adapt the ADM to my enterprise?
- Why does the ADM process need to be governed?
- What are the major information areas covered by a governance repository?
- What are the reasons for scoping the architecture activity for my organization?
- What are the possible dimensions for limiting the scope?
- Why is there a need for an integration framework that sits above individual architectures?

## 5.2 The Architecture Development Cycle

*(Syllabus Reference: Unit 4, Learning Outcome 1: You should be able to briefly describe the ADM cycle, its phases and the objective of each phase.)*

The ADM consists of a number of phases that cycle through a range of architecture domains that enable the architect to ensure that a complex set of requirements is adequately addressed. The basic structure of the ADM is shown in Figure 9.

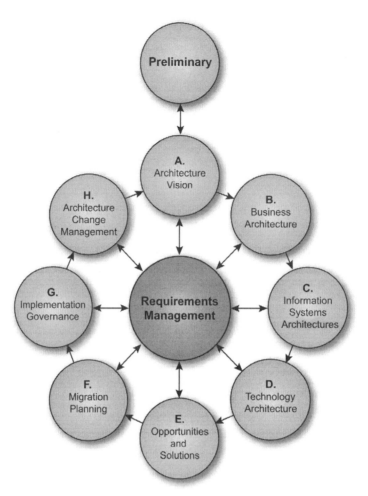

Figure 9: The Architecture Development Method Cycle

The ADM is applied iteratively throughout the entire process, between phases, and within them. Throughout the ADM cycle, there should be frequent validation of results against the original requirements, both those for the whole ADM cycle, and those for the particular phase of the process. Such validation should reconsider scope, detail, schedules, and milestones. Each phase should consider assets produced from previous iterations of the process and external assets from the marketplace, such as other frameworks or models.

The ADM supports the concept of iteration at three levels:

- **Cycling around the ADM**: The ADM is presented in a circular manner indicating that the completion of one phase of architecture work directly feeds into subsequent phases of architecture work.
- **Iterating between phases**: TOGAF describes the concept of iterating across phases (e.g., returning to Business Architecture on completion of Technology Architecture).
- **Cycling around a single phase**: TOGAF supports repeated execution of the activities within a single ADM phase as a technique for elaborating architectural content.

A summary of the objectives is shown in Table 7.

Table 7:    Architecture Development Method Activity by Phase

| ADM Phase | Objectives |
|---|---|
| Preliminary Phase | Prepare the organization for successful TOGAF architecture projects. Undertake the preparation and initiation activities required to create an Architecture Capability, including the customization of TOGAF, selection of tools, and the definition of Architecture Principles. |
| Requirements Management | Every stage of a TOGAF project is based on and validates business requirements. Requirements are identified, stored, and fed into and out of the relevant ADM phases, which dispose of, address, and prioritize requirements. |
| Phase A: Architecture Vision | Set the scope, constraints, and expectations for a TOGAF project. Create the Architecture Vision. Identify stakeholders. Validate the business context and create the Statement of Architecture Work. Obtain approvals. |
| Phase B: Business Architecture Phase C: Information Systems Architectures (Application & Data) Phase D: Technology Architecture | Develop architectures in four domains: 1. Business 2. Information Systems – Application 3. Information Systems – Data 4. Technology In each case, develop the Baseline and Target Architecture and analyze gaps. |
| Phase E: Opportunities & Solutions | Perform initial implementation planning and the identification of delivery vehicles for the building blocks identified in the previous phases. Determine whether an incremental approach is required, and if so identify Transition Architectures. |

| ADM Phase | Objectives |
|---|---|
| Phase F: Migration Planning | Develop detailed Implementation and Migration Plan that addresses how to move from the Baseline to the Target Architecture. |
| Phase G: Implementation Governance | Provide architectural oversight for the implementation. Prepare and issue Architecture Contracts. Ensure that the implementation project conforms to the architecture. |
| Phase H: Architecture Change Management | Provide continual monitoring and a change management process to ensure that the architecture responds to the needs of the enterprise and maximizes the value of the architecture to the business. |

**Scoping an Enterprise Architecture Activity**

The ADM defines a recommended sequence for the various phases and steps involved in developing an organization-wide enterprise architecture, but does not determine the scope for an enterprise architecture activity; this must be determined by the organization itself.

*(Syllabus Reference: Unit 4, Learning Outcome 2: You should be able to describe a typical set of steps.)*

The phases of the ADM cycle are further divided into steps; for example, the steps within the Business Architecture phase are as follows:

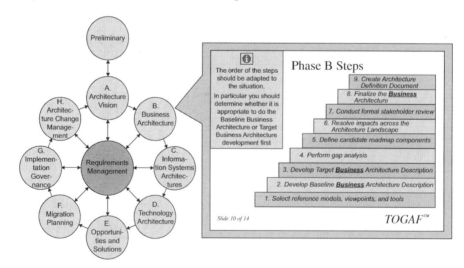

The steps shown are uniform for Phases B, C, and D.

TOGAF 9 Foundation does not go into the detail of the contents of the steps within the ADM phases. That is a topic for the Level 2, TOGAF 9 Certified.

*(Syllabus Reference: Unit 4, Learning Outcome 3: You should be able to describe the versioning convention for deliverables used in Phases A to D.)*

Throughout the process of applying the ADM, outputs are generated. An output in an early phase may be modified in a later phase. The versioning of output is managed through version numbers.

In particular, a version numbering convention is used within the ADM to illustrate the evolution of Baseline and Target Architecture Definitions, as follows:

| Phase | Deliverable | Content | Version | Description |
|---|---|---|---|---|
| A: Architecture Vision | Architecture Vision | Business Architecture | 0.1 | Version 0.1 indicates that a high-level outline of the architecture is in place. |
| | | Data Architecture | 0.1 | |
| | | Application Architecture | 0.1 | |
| | | Technology Architecture | 0.1 | |
| B: Business Architecture | Architecture Definition Document | Business Architecture | 1.0 | Version 1.0 indicates a formally reviewed, detailed architecture. |
| C: Information Systems Architecture | Architecture Definition Document | Data Architecture | 1.0 | |
| | | Application Architecture | 1.0 | |
| D: Technology Architecture | Architecture Definition Document | Technology Architecture | 1.0 | |

**ADM Output Versioning**

The numbering scheme provided in the TOGAF ADM for its outputs is intended as an example. It should be adapted by the architect to meet the requirements of the organization and to work with the architecture tools and repositories employed by the organization.

## 5.3 What is the Relationship of the ADM to Other Parts of TOGAF?

*(Syllabus Reference: Unit 4, Learning Outcome 4: You should be able to describe the relationship between the ADM and other parts of TOGAF – the Enterprise Continuum, Architecture Repository, Foundation Architecture, and Supporting Guidelines and Techniques.)*

This section explains the relationship between the ADM and other parts of TOGAF.

### 5.3.1 Relationship to the Enterprise Continuum and Architecture Repository

The Enterprise Continuum is an approach for categorizing architectural source material – both the contents of the organization's own Architecture Repository, and the set of relevant, available reference models in the industry. The practical implementation of the Enterprise Continuum will typically take the form of an Architecture Repository that includes reference architectures, models, and patterns that have been accepted for use within the enterprise, and actual architectural work done previously within the enterprise.

At relevant places throughout the ADM, there are reminders to consider which architecture assets from the Architecture Repository the architect should use, if any. In some cases – for example, in the development of a Technology Architecture – this may be the TOGAF Foundation Architecture. Similarly, in the development of a Business Architecture, it may be a reference model for e-Commerce taken from the industry at large.

While using the ADM, the architect is developing a snapshot of the enterprise's decisions and their implications at particular points in time. Each iteration of the ADM will populate an organization-specific landscape with all the architecture assets identified and leveraged through the process, including the final organization-specific architecture delivered.

Architecture development is a continuous, cyclical process, and in executing the ADM repeatedly over time, the architect gradually adds more and more content to the organization's Architecture Repository. Although the primary focus of the ADM is on the development of the enterprise-specific architecture, in this wider context the ADM can also be viewed as the process of populating the enterprise's own Architecture Repository with relevant re-usable building blocks taken from the "left", more generic side of the Enterprise Continuum.

In fact, the first execution of the ADM will often be the hardest, since the architecture assets available for re-use will be relatively scarce. Even at this stage of development, however, there will be architecture assets available from external sources such as TOGAF, as well as the IT industry at large, that could be leveraged in support of the effort.

Subsequent executions will be easier, as more and more architecture assets become identified, are used to populate the organization's Architecture Repository, and are thus available for future re-use.

### 5.3.2 The ADM and the Foundation Architecture

The ADM is also useful when populating the Foundation Architecture of an enterprise. Business requirements of an enterprise may be used to identify the necessary definitions and selections in the Foundation Architecture. This could be a set of re-usable common models, policy and governance definitions, or even as specific as overriding technology selections (e.g., if mandated by law). Population of the Foundation Architecture follows similar principles as for an enterprise architecture, with the difference that requirements for a whole enterprise are restricted to the overall concerns and thus less complete than for a specific enterprise.

### 5.3.3 The ADM and Supporting Guidelines and Techniques

*(Syllabus Reference: Unit 4, Learning Outcome 5: You should be able to explain the purpose of the supporting guidelines and techniques, and the difference between guidelines and techniques.)*

TOGAF 9 Part III: ADM Guidelines and Techniques is a set of resources – guidelines, templates, checklists, and other detailed materials – that directly support application of the TOGAF ADM.

The individual guidelines and techniques are described in a separate part of TOGAF so that they can be referenced from the relevant points in the ADM as necessary, rather than having the detailed text clutter the description of the ADM itself.

**Guidelines versus Technique**

The guidelines provided with TOGAF describe how the ADM process can be adapted to deal with a number of different usage scenarios, including different process styles (e.g., the use of iteration) and also specific specialty architectures (such as security).

The techniques described within TOGAF 9 Part III support specific tasks within the ADM (e.g., the gap analysis technique, principles, etc.).

## 5.4  Key Points of the ADM Cycle

*(Syllabus Reference: Unit 4, Learning Outcome 6: You should be able to briefly explain the key points of the ADM cycle.)*

The TOGAF ADM is iterative. New decisions have to be taken at each iteration:

1. Enterprise coverage
2. Level of detail
3. Time period
4. Architecture asset re-use:
   — Previous ADM iterations
   — Other frameworks, system models, industry models, …

Decisions taken should be based on competence and/or resource availability, and the value accruing to the enterprise.

The ADM does not recommend the scope of activity; this has to be determined by the organization itself.

The choice of scope is critical to the success of the architecting effort. The main guideline is to focus on what creates value to the enterprise, and to select horizontal and vertical scope, and project schedules, accordingly. This exercise will be repeated, and future iterations will build on what is being created in the current effort, adding greater width and depth.

Where necessary, use of the ADM should be tailored to meet the needs of the organization. This means that some phases may be omitted, modified, or even additional procedures added.

## 5.5  How to Adapt the ADM to your Enterprise

*(Syllabus Reference: Unit 4, Learning Outcome 7: You should be able to list the main reasons why you would need to adapt the ADM.)*

The ADM is a generic method for architecture development, which is designed to deal with most system and organizational requirements. It easily copes with variable geographies, vertical sectors, and industry types. However, it will often be necessary to modify or extend the ADM to suit specific needs. One of the tasks before applying the ADM is to review the process and its outputs for applicability, and then tailor them as appropriate to the circumstances of the individual enterprise. This activity may well produce an "enterprise-specific" ADM.

There are a number of reasons for wanting to tailor the ADM to the circumstances of an individual enterprise. Some of the reasons are outlined as follows:

1.  An important consideration is that the order of the phases in the ADM is to some extent dependent on the maturity of the architecture discipline within the enterprise concerned. For example, if the business case for doing architecture is not well recognized, then creating an Architecture Vision is essential; and a detailed Business Architecture needs to come next to define the business case for the remaining architecture work, and secure the active participation of key stakeholders in that work.

2.  The order of phases may also be defined by the business and architecture principles of an enterprise. For example, the business principles may dictate that the enterprise be prepared to adjust its business processes to meet the needs of a packaged solution, so that it can be implemented quickly to enable fast response to market changes. In such a case, the Business Architecture (or at least the completion of it) may well follow completion of the Information Systems Architecture.

3.  An enterprise may wish to use or tailor the ADM in conjunction with another enterprise architecture framework that has a defined set of deliverables specific to a particular vertical sector: Government, Defense, e-Business, Telecommunications, etc.

4.  The ADM is one of many corporate processes that make up the corporate governance model for an enterprise. The ADM is complementary to, and supportive of, other standard program management processes. The enterprise will tailor the ADM to reflect the relationships with, and dependencies on, the other management processes.

5.  The ADM is being mandated for use by a prime or lead contractor in an outsourcing situation, and needs to be tailored to achieve a suitable compromise between the contractor's existing practices and the contracting enterprise's requirements.

6.  The enterprise is a small-to-medium enterprise, and wishes to use a "cut-down" version of the ADM that is more attuned to the reduced level of resources and system complexity typical of such an environment.

7.  The enterprise is very large and complex, comprising many separate but interlinked "enterprises" within an overall collaborative business framework, and the architecture method needs to be adapted to recognize this. Such enterprises usually cannot be treated successfully as a single entity and a more federated approach is required.

The ADM process can also be adapted to deal with a number of different use scenarios, including different process styles (e.g., the use of iteration) and also specific specialist architectures (such as security). These are discussed in Chapter 8.

## 5.6  The Need for Architecture Governance

*(Syllabus Reference: Unit 4, Learning Outcome 8: You should be able to explain the need for the ADM process to be governed.)*

The ADM, whether adapted by the organization or used as documented in TOGAF, is a key process to be managed and governed. The Architecture Board should be satisfied that the method is being applied correctly across all phases of an architecture development iteration. Compliance with the ADM is fundamental to the governance of the architecture, to ensure that all considerations are made and all required deliverables are produced.

*(Syllabus Reference: Unit 4, Learning Outcome 9: You should be able to describe the major information areas managed by a governance repository.)*

The management of all architectural artifacts, governance, and related processes should be supported by a controlled environment. Typically this would be based on one or more repositories supporting versioned object and process control and status.

The major information areas managed by a governance repository should contain the following types of information:

- **Reference Data** (collateral from the organization's own repositories/ Enterprise Continuum, including external data; e.g., COBIT, ITIL): Used for guidance and instruction during project implementation. This includes the details of information outlined above. The reference data includes a description of the governance procedures themselves.
- **Process Status**: A record of all information regarding the state of any governance processes; examples of this include outstanding compliance requests, dispensation requests, and compliance assessment investigations.
- **Audit Information**: A record of all completed governance process actions. This is used to support:
  — Key decisions and responsible personnel for any architecture project that has been sanctioned by the governance process
  — A reference for future architectural and supporting process developments, guidance, and precedence

## 5.7  Scoping the Architecture Activity for your Organization

*(Syllabus Reference: Unit 4, Learning Outcome 10: You should be able to briefly explain the reasons for scoping an architecture activity.)*

There are many reasons to constrain (or restrict) the scope of the architectural activity to be undertaken, most of which relate to limits in:

- The organizational authority of the team producing the architecture
- The objectives and stakeholder concerns to be addressed within the architecture
- The availability of people, finance, and other resources

The scope chosen for the architecture activity is normally directly dependent on available resources, and, in the final analysis, is usually a question of feasibility.

*(Syllabus Reference: Unit 4, Learning Outcome 11: You should be able to list the possible dimensions for limiting the scope of an architecture activity.)*

Table 8 shows the four dimensions in which the scope may be defined and limited.

Table 8:    Dimensions for Limiting the Scope of the Architecture Activitity

| Dimension | Considerations |
| --- | --- |
| Breadth | What is the full extent of the enterprise, and what part of that extent should the architecting effort deal with? Many enterprises are very large, effectively comprising a federation of organizational units that could validly be considered enterprises in their own right. The modern enterprise increasingly extends beyond its traditional boundaries, to embrace a fuzzy combination of traditional business enterprise combined with suppliers, customers, and partners. |
| Depth | To what level of detail should the architecting effort go? How much architecture is "enough"? What is the appropriate demarcation between the architecture effort and other, related activities (system design, system engineering, system development)? |
| Time period | What is the time period that needs to be articulated for the Architecture Vision, and does it make sense (in terms of practicality and resources) for the same period to be covered in the detailed architecture description? If not, how many Transition Architectures are to be defined, and what are their time periods? |
| Architecture domains | A complete enterprise architecture description should contain all four architecture domains (Business, Data, Application, Technology), but the realities of resource and time constraints often mean there is not enough time, funding, or resources to build a top-down, all-inclusive architecture description encompassing all four architecture domains, even if the enterprise scope is chosen to be less than the full extent of the overall enterprise. |

Typically, the scope of an architecture is first expressed in terms of breadth, depth, and time. Once these dimensions are understood, a suitable combination of architecture domains can be selected that are appropriate to the problem being addressed.

## 5.8 Integrating the Architecture Domains for your Organization

*(Syllabus Reference: Unit 4, Learning Outcome 12: You should be able to briefly explain the need for an integration framework that sits above individual architectures.)*

Architectures that are created to address a subset of issues within an enterprise require a consistent frame of reference so that they can be considered as a group as well as point deliverables. The dimensions that are used to define the scope boundary of a single architecture (e.g., level of detail, architecture domain, etc.) are typically the same dimensions that must be addressed when considering the integration of many architectures. Figure 10 illustrates how different types of architecture need to co-exist.

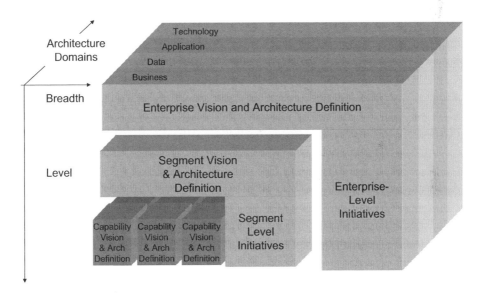

Figure 10:    Integration of Architecture Artifacts

At the present time, the state-of-the-art is such that architecture integration can only be accomplished at the lower end of the integration spectrum. Key factors to consider are the granularity and level of detail in each artifact, and the maturity of standards for the interchange of architectural descriptions.

## 5.9  Summary

The TOGAF ADM is a comprehensive general method that defines a recommended sequence for the various phases and steps involved in developing an architecture. It is an iterative method. A number of inputs and outputs are recommended for each phase. It draws on other parts of TOGAF for assets and processes. The ADM can be used with other deliverables from other frameworks.

The ADM does not recommend a scope; this has to be determined by the organization itself. The choice of scope is critical to the success of the architecting effort. The main guideline is to focus on what creates value to the enterprise, and to select horizontal and vertical scope, and project schedules, accordingly. This exercise will be repeated, and future iterations will build on what is being created in the current effort, adding greater width and depth.

Where necessary, use of the ADM should be tailored to meet the needs of the organization. This means that some phases may be omitted, modified, or even additional procedures added.

## 5.10  Test Yourself Questions

Q1:  Complete the sentence: Phase H _____
   A.  Prepares the organization for successful TOGAF architecture projects
   B.  Develops Baseline and Target Architectures and analyzes the gaps
   C.  Prepares and issues Architecture Contracts
   D.  Ensures that the architecture responds to the needs of the enterprise
   E.  All of these

Q2:  Which of the following is the final step in development of the four architecture domains?
   A.  Conduct formal stakeholder review
   B.  Create Architecture Definition Document
   C.  Perform gap analysis
   D.  Select reference models, viewpoints, and tools

Q3:   Which of the following version numbers is used by TOGAF as a convention to denote a high-level outline of an architecture?
   A.   Version 0
   B.   Version 0.1
   C.   Version 0.5
   D.   Version 1.0

Q4:   Which one of the following does not complete the sentence: When executing the ADM, the architect is not only developing a snapshot of the enterprise, but is also populating the _____
   A.   Architecture Repository
   B.   Architecture Capability Framework
   C.   Enterprise Continuum
   D.   Foundation Architecture

Q5:   Which of the following statements does not describe the phases of the ADM?
   A.   They are cyclical.
   B.   They are iterative.
   C.   Each phase refines the scope.
   D.   Each phase is mandatory.
   E.   They cycle through a range of architecture views.

Q6:   Which one of the following best describes a reason to adapt the ADM and take a federated approach?
   A.   The maturity of the architecture discipline within the enterprise
   B.   The use of the ADM in conjunction with another enterprise framework
   C.   The ADM is being used by a lead contractor in an outsourcing situation
   D.   The enterprise is very large and complex

Q7:   Which of the following are the major information areas managed by a
      governance repository?
      A.   Foundation Architectures, Industry Architectures, Organization-
           Specific Architectures
      B.   Standards Information Base, Architecture Landscape, Governance
           Log
      C.   Reference Data, Process Status, Audit Information
      D.   Application Architecture, Business Architecture, Data Architecture

Q8:   Which of these is *not* considered a dimension to consider when setting
      the scope of the architecture activity?
      A.   Architecture Domains
      B.   Breadth
      C.   Depth
      D.   Data Architecture
      E.   Time Period

## 5.11  Recommended Reading

The following are recommended sources of further information for this
chapter:

- TOGAF 9 Part II: ADM, Chapter 5 (Introduction)

# Chapter 6

# The Enterprise Continuum and Tools

## 6.1 Key Learning Points

This chapter will help you understand the Enterprise Continuum, its purpose, and constituent parts. It also introduces the topic of tools standardization.

**Key Points Explained**

This chapter will help you to answer the following questions:

- What is the Enterprise Continuum?
- How is the Enterprise Continuum used in developing an architecture?
- How does the Enterprise Continuum promote re-use of architecture artifacts?
- What are the constituent pieces of the Enterprise Continuum?
- What is the Architecture Continuum?
- How is the Architecture Continuum used in developing an architecture?
- What is the relationship between the Architecture Continuum and the Solutions Continuum?
- What is the Solutions Continuum?
- How is the Solutions Continuum used to develop an architecture?
- What is the relationship between the Enterprise Continuum and the ADM?
- What is the Architecture Repository?
- What are the high-level issues with tools standardization?

**Definition of "Continuum"**

Noun: a continuous extent of something, no part of which is different from any other.

[Source: Wiktionary.org]

## 6.2  Overview of the Enterprise Continuum

*(Syllabus Reference: Unit 5, Learning Outcome 1: You should be able to briefly explain what the Enterprise Continuum is.)*

The Enterprise Continuum provides methods for classifying architecture and solution artifacts, both internal and external to the Architecture Repository, as they evolve from generic Foundation Architectures to Organization-Specific Architectures.

*(Syllabus Reference: Unit 5, Learning Outcome 2: You should be able to explain how the Enterprise Continuum is used in organizing and developing an architecture.)*

The Enterprise Continuum enables the architect to articulate the broad perspective of what, why, and how the enterprise architecture has been designed with the factors and drivers considered. The Enterprise Continuum is an important aid to communication and understanding, both within individual enterprises, and between customer enterprises and vendor organizations. Without an understanding of "where in the continuum you are", people discussing architecture can often talk at cross-purposes because they are referencing different points in the continuum at the same time, without realizing it.

**The Benefits of a Consistent Language**

Any architecture is context-specific; for example, there are architectures that are specific to individual customers, industries, subsystems, products, and services. Architects, on both the buy-side and supply-side, must have at their disposal a consistent language to effectively communicate the differences between architectures. Such a language enables engineering efficiency and the effective use of Commercial Off-The-Shelf (COTS) product functionality. The Enterprise Continuum provides that consistent language.

## 6.3  The Enterprise Continuum and Architecture Re-Use

*(Syllabus Reference: Unit 5, Learning Outcome 3: You should be able to explain how the Enterprise Continuum promotes re-use of architecture artifacts.)*

The Enterprise Continuum enables the organization of re-usable architecture artifacts and solution assets to maximize the enterprise architecture investment opportunities.

The "virtual repository" that is the Enterprise Continuum consists of all the architecture assets; that is, models, patterns, architecture descriptions, and other artifacts produced during application of the ADM. These can exist both within the enterprise and in the IT industry at large, and are considered the set of assets available for the development of architectures for the enterprise.

The deliverables of previous architecture work, which are available for re-use, are examples of internal architecture and solutions artifacts. Examples of external architecture and solution artifacts include the wide variety of industry reference models and architecture patterns that exist, and are continually emerging, including those that are highly generic (such as TOGAF's own Technical Reference Model (TRM)); those specific to certain aspects of IT (such as a web services architecture); those specific to certain types of information processing (such as e-Commerce); and those specific to certain vertical industries, such as the models generated by vertical consortia like the TMF (in the Telecommunications sector), ARTS (Retail), Energistics (Petrotechnical), etc.

The enterprise architecture determines which architecture and solution artifacts an organization includes in its Architecture Repository. Re-use is a major consideration in this decision.

## 6.4 The Constituent Parts of the Enterprise Continuum

*(Syllabus Reference: Unit 5, Learning Outcome 4: You should be able to describe the constituent parts of the Enterprise Continuum.)*

The Enterprise Continuum consists of three parts as described below, and illustrated in Figure 6. Each of the three parts is considered to be a distinct continuum.

### 6.4.1 The Enterprise Continuum

*(Syllabus Reference: Unit 5, Learning Outcome 5: You should be able to explain the purpose of the Enterprise Continuum.)*

The Enterprise Continuum is the outermost continuum and classifies assets related to the context of the overall enterprise architecture.

The Enterprise Continuum classes of assets may influence architectures, but are not directly used during the ADM architecture development. The Enterprise Continuum classifies contextual assets used to develop architectures, such as policies, standards, strategic initiatives, organizational structures, and enterprise-level capabilities. The Enterprise Continuum can also classify solutions (as opposed to descriptions or specifications of solutions). Finally, the Enterprise Continuum contains two specializations, namely the Architecture and Solutions continuum.

### 6.4.2   The Architecture Continuum

The Architecture Continuum offers a consistent way to define and understand the generic rules, representations, and relationships in an architecture, including traceability and derivation relationships (e.g., to show that an Organization-Specific Architecture is based on an industry or generic standard).

The Architecture Continuum represents a structuring of Architecture Building Blocks (ABBs) which are re-usable architecture assets. ABBs evolve through their development lifecycle from abstract and generic entities to fully expressed Organization-Specific Architecture assets. The Architecture Continuum assets will be used to guide and select the elements in the Solutions Continuum (see below).

The Architecture Continuum shows the relationships among foundational frameworks (such as TOGAF), common system architectures (such as the III-RM), industry architectures, and enterprise architectures. The Architecture Continuum is a useful tool to discover commonality and eliminate unnecessary redundancy.

### 6.4.3   The Solutions Continuum

The Solutions Continuum provides a consistent way to describe and understand the implementation of the assets defined in the Architecture Continuum. The Solutions Continuum defines what is available in the organizational environment as re-usable Solution Building Blocks (SBBs). The solutions are the results of agreements between customers and business partners that implement the rules and relationships defined in the architecture space. The Solutions Continuum addresses the commonalities and differences among the products, systems, and services of implemented systems.

## 6.5  The Architecture Continuum in Detail

*(Syllabus Reference: Unit 5, Learning Outcome 6: You should be able to explain the purpose of the Architecture Continuum.)*

There is a continuum of architectures, Architecture Building Blocks (ABBs), and architecture models that are relevant to the task of constructing an enterprise-specific architecture, that are termed by TOGAF as the Architecture Continuum. These are shown in Figure 11.

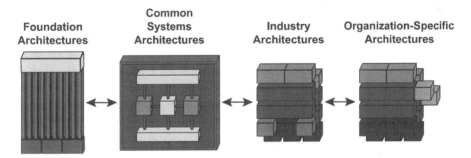

Figure 11:    The Architecture Continuum

*(Syllabus Reference: Unit 5, Learning Outcome 7: You should be able to list the stages of architecture evolution defined in the Architecture Continuum.)*

Figure 11 illustrates how architectures are developed and evolved across a continuum ranging from Foundation Architectures, such as the one provided by TOGAF, through Common Systems Architectures, and Industry Architectures, and to an enterprise's own Organization-Specific Architectures.

The arrows in the Architecture Continuum represent the relationship that exists between the different architectures in the Architecture Continuum. The leftwards direction focuses on meeting enterprise needs and business requirements, while the rightwards direction focuses on leveraging architectural components and building blocks.

The enterprise needs and business requirements are addressed in increasing detail from left to right. The architect will typically look to find re-usable architecture elements toward the left of the continuum. When elements are not found, the requirements for the missing elements are passed to the left of the continuum for incorporation.

Within the Architecture Continuum there are a number of re-usable Architecture Building Blocks (ABBs) – the models of architectures.

### 6.5.1 Foundation Architecture

A Foundation Architecture consists of generic components, inter-relationships, principles, and guidelines that provide a foundation on which more specific architectures can be built.

### 6.5.2 Common Systems Architectures

Common Systems Architectures guide the selection and integration of specific services from the Foundation Architecture to create an architecture useful for building common solutions across a wide number of relevant domains. Examples of Common Systems Architectures include Security Architecture, Management Architecture, Network Architecture, etc.

The TOGAF Integrated Information Infrastructure Reference Model (III-RM) is a reference model that supports describing Common Systems Architecture in the Application domain that focuses on the requirements, building blocks, and standards relating to the vision of Boundaryless Information Flow.

### 6.5.3 Industry Architectures

Industry Architectures guide the integration of common systems components with industry-specific components, and guide the creation of industry solutions for specific customer problems within a particular industry.

A typical example of an industry-specific component is a data model representing the business functions and processes specific to a particular vertical industry, such as the Retail industry's "Active Store" architecture, or an Industry Architecture that incorporates the Petrotechnical Open Software Corporation (POSC) (www.posc.org) data model.

### 6.5.4 Organization-Specific Architectures

Organization-Specific Architectures describe and guide the final deployment of user-written or third-party components that constitute effective solutions for particular enterprises.

## 6.6 The Solutions Continuum in Detail

*(Syllabus Reference: Unit 5, Learning Outcome 8: You should be able to explain the purpose of the Solutions Continuum.)*

The Solutions Continuum, shown in Figure 12, represents the implementations of the architectures at the corresponding levels of the Architecture Continuum. At each level in the Solutions Continuum there is a set of reference building blocks that represent a solution to the business requirements at that level. A populated Solutions Continuum can be regarded as a re-use library.

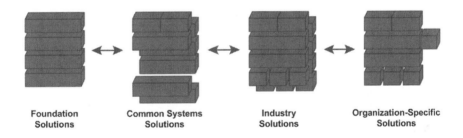

|  |  |  |  |
|---|---|---|---|
| Foundation Solutions | Common Systems Solutions | Industry Solutions | Organization-Specific Solutions |

Figure 12:   The Solutions Continuum

In Figure 12, moving from left-to-right increases the solution's value; that is, products and services provide value in creating systems solutions. Systems solutions value is used to create industry solutions, and industry solutions are used to create enterprise solutions (also termed customer solutions). The right-to-left direction increasingly focuses on addressing enterprise needs.

*(Syllabus Reference: Unit 5, Learning Outcome 9: You should be able to list the stages of architecture evolution defined in the Solutions Continuum.)*

The solution types within the Solutions Continuum are looked at in detail in the following sections.

### 6.6.1  Foundation Solutions

Foundation Solutions are highly generic concepts, tools, products, services, and solution components that are the fundamental providers of capabilities. Services include professional services – such as training and consulting services – that ensure the maximum investment value from solutions in the shortest possible time; and support services – such as Help Desk – that ensure the maximum possible value from solutions (services that ensure timely updates and upgrades to the products and systems).

Example Foundation Solutions would include programming languages, operating systems, foundational data structures (such as EDIFACT), generic approaches to organization structuring, foundational structures for organizing IT operations (such as ITIL), etc.

### 6.6.2  Common Systems Solutions

A Common Systems Solution is an implementation of a Common Systems Architecture and is comprised of a set of products and services, which may be certified or branded. It represents the highest common denominator for one or more solutions in the industry segments that the Common Systems Solution supports.

Common Systems Solutions represent collections of common requirements and capabilities, rather than those specific to a particular customer or industry. Common Systems Solutions provide organizations with operating environments specific to operational and informational needs, such as high availability transaction processing and scalable data warehousing systems. Examples of Common Systems Solutions include: an enterprise management system product and a security system product.

Computer systems vendors are the typical providers of technology-centric Common Systems Solutions. "Software as a service" vendors are typical providers of common application solutions. Business process outsourcing vendors are typical providers of business capability-centric Common Systems Solutions.

### 6.6.3  Industry Solutions

An Industry Solution is an implementation of an Industry Architecture, which provides re-usable packages of common components and services specific to an industry.

Fundamental components are provided by Common Systems Solutions and/or Foundation Solutions, and are augmented with industry-specific components. Examples include a physical database schema or an industry-specific point-of-service device.

Industry Solutions are industry-specific, aggregate procurements that are ready to be tailored to an individual organization's requirements.

In some cases an industry solution may include not only an implementation of the Industry Architecture, but also other solution elements, such as specific products, services, and systems solutions that are appropriate to that industry.

### 6.6.4 Organization-Specific Solutions

An Organization-Specific Solution is an implementation of the Organization-Specific Architecture that provides the required business functions. Because solutions are designed for specific business operations, they contain the highest amount of unique content in order to accommodate the varying people and processes of specific organizations.

Building Organization-Specific Solutions on Industry Solutions, Common Systems Solutions, and Foundation Solutions is the usual way of connecting the Architecture Continuum to the Solutions Continuum, as guided by the architects within an enterprise.

An Organization-Specific Solution will be structured in order to support specific Service-Level Agreements (SLAs) to ensure support of the operational systems at desired service levels. For example, a third-party application hosting provider may offer different levels of support for operational systems. These agreements would define the terms and conditions of that support.

Other key factors to be defined within an Organization-Specific Solution are the key operating parameters and quality metrics that can be used to monitor and manage the environment.

### 6.6.5   The Relationship of the Architecture Continuum to the Solutions Continuum

The relationship between the Architecture Continuum and the Solutions Continuum is one of guidance, direction, and support. For example, Foundation Architectures guide the creation or selection of Foundation Solutions. Foundation Solutions support the Foundation Architecture by helping to realize the architecture defined in the Architecture Continuum. The Foundation Architecture also guides development of Foundation Solutions, by providing architectural direction, requirements and principles that guide selection, and realization of appropriate solutions. A similar relationship exists between the other elements of the Enterprise Continuum.

The relationships depicted in Figure 13 are a best case for the ideal use of architecture and solution components.

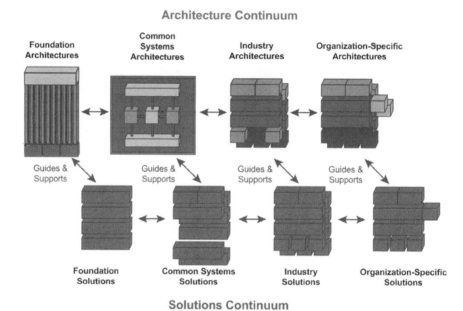

Figure 13:   The Enterprise Continuum

## 6.7  Using the Enterprise Continuum within the ADM

*(Syllabus Reference: Unit 5, Learning Outcome 10: You should be able to explain the relationship between the Enterprise Continuum and the TOGAF ADM.)*

The TOGAF Architecture Development Method (ADM) describes the process of moving from the TOGAF Foundation Architecture to an enterprise-specific architecture (or set of architectures). This process makes use of the elements of the TOGAF Foundation Architecture and other relevant architecture assets, components, and building blocks. At relevant places throughout the TOGAF ADM, there are reminders to consider which architecture assets from the Enterprise Continuum the architect should use. TOGAF itself provides two reference models for consideration for inclusion in an organization's Enterprise Continuum: the TOGAF Foundation Architecture and the Integrated Information Infrastructure Reference Model (III-RM).

## 6.8  The Architecture Repository

*(Syllabus Reference: Unit 5, Learning Outcome 11: You should be able to describe the Architecture Repository.)*

Operating a mature architecture capability within a large enterprise creates a huge volume of architectural output. Effective management and leverage of these architectural work products require a formal taxonomy for different types of architectural asset alongside dedicated processes and tools for architectural content storage.

TOGAF provides a structural framework for an Architecture Repository that allows an enterprise to distinguish between different types of architectural assets that exist at different levels of abstraction in the organization. This Architecture Repository is one part of the wider Enterprise Repository, which provides the capability to link architectural assets to components of the Detailed Design, Deployment, and Service Management Repositories.

*(Syllabus Reference: Unit 5, Learning Outcome 12: You should be able to explain the relationship between the Enterprise Continuum and the Architecture Repository.)*

The Architecture Repository is a model for a physical instance of the Enterprise Continuum.

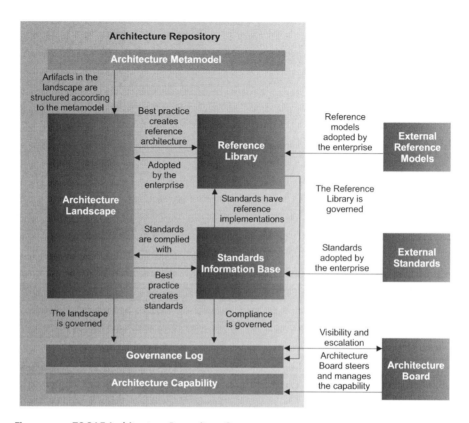

Figure 14:   TOGAF Architecture Repository Structure

*(Syllabus Reference: Unit 5, Learning Outcome 13: You should be able to describe the classes of information held in the Architecture Repository.)*

At a high level, six classes of architectural information are expected to be held within an Architecture Repository:

- The **Architecture Metamodel** describes the organizationally tailored application of an architecture framework, including a method for architecture development and a metamodel for architecture content.
- The **Architecture Capability** defines the parameters, structures, and processes that support governance of the Architecture Repository.
- The **Architecture Landscape** presents an architectural representation of assets in use, or planned, by the enterprise at particular points in time.
- The **Standards Information Base** captures the standards with which new architectures must comply, which may include industry standards, selected products and services from suppliers, or shared services already

deployed within the organization. The Open Group provides an example of a Standards Information Base on its web site.[9]

- The **Reference Library** provides guidelines, templates, patterns, and other forms of reference material that can be leveraged in order to accelerate the creation of new architectures for the enterprise.
- The **Governance Log** provides a record of governance activity across the enterprise.

### 6.8.1 The Architecture Landscape

*(Syllabus Reference: Unit 5, Learning Outcome 14: You should be able to list the three levels of the Architecture Landscape.)*

The Architecture Landscape holds architectural views of the state of the enterprise at particular points in time. Due to the sheer volume and the diverse stakeholder needs throughout an entire enterprise, the Architecture Landscape is divided into three levels of granularity:

1. Strategic Architectures show a long-term summary view of the entire enterprise. Strategic Architectures provide an organizing framework for operational and change activity and allow for direction setting at an executive level.
2. Segment Architectures provide more detailed operating models for areas within an enterprise. Segment Architectures can be used at the program or portfolio level to organize and operationally align more detailed change activity.
3. Capability Architectures show in a more detailed fashion how the enterprise can support a particular unit of capability. Capability Architectures are used to provide an overview of current capability, target capability, and capability increments and allow for individual work packages and projects to be grouped within managed portfolios and programs.

### 6.8.2 The Standards Information Base

*(Syllabus Reference: Unit 5, Learning Outcome 15: You should be able to explain the purpose of the Standards Information Base within the Architecture Repository.)*

---

9    Go to www.opengroup.org/sib.

The Standards Information Base is a repository area that can hold a set of specifications, to which architectures must conform.

Establishment of a Standards Information Base provides an unambiguous basis for architectural governance since:
- The standards are easily accessible to projects and therefore the obligations of the project can be understood and planned for.
- Standards are stated in a clear and unambiguous manner, so that compliance can be objectively as

## 6.9 Tools Standardization

To manage the content of the Enterprise Continuum we need tools in order to:
- Promote re-use
- Enable sharing of architecture information within an organization
- Facilitate easier maintenance of the architecture
- Ensure common terminology is used
- Provide stakeholders with relevant models

Using the models within TOGAF, it is then possible to implement the Architecture Repository in a tool, thereby responding to stakeholder enquiries for models, views, and other queries.

## 6.10 Summary

The Enterprise Continuum provides methods for classifying architecture and solution artifacts, both internal and external to the Architecture Repository, as they evolve from generic Foundation Architectures to Organization-Specific Architectures. It is also an aid to communication between all architects involved in building and procuring an architecture by providing a common language and terminology. This, in turn, enables efficiency in engineering and effective use of COTS products.

The Architecture Continuum is part of an organization's Enterprise Continuum and is supported by the Solutions Continuum. It offers a consistent way to define and understand the generic rules, representations, and relationships in an information system, and it represents a conceptual structuring of re-usable architecture assets.

The Architecture Continuum shows the relationships among Foundation Architectures (such as the TOGAF Foundation Architecture), Common Systems Architectures (such as the III-RM), Industry Architectures, and Organization-Specific Architectures. It is also a useful method to discover commonality and eliminate unnecessary redundancy.

The Solutions Continuum is part of an organization's Enterprise Continuum. It represents implementations of the architectures at the corresponding levels of the Architecture Continuum. At each level, the Solutions Continuum is a population of the architecture with reference building blocks – either purchased products or built components – that represent a solution to the enterprise's business needs.

The Architecture Repository provides a structural framework for a physical repository for managing architectural work products and is a model of a physical instance of the Enterprise Continuum. The Architecture Repository defines six classes for architectural information held in the repository.

TOGAF recognizes the need to manage the content of the Enterprise Continuum using tools, and includes high-level guidance on standardization of tools.

## 6.11  Test Yourself Questions

Q1:  Which of the following statements does *not* apply to the Enterprise Continuum?

A.  It is a repository of all known architecture assets and artifacts in the IT industry.

B.  It is a view of the Architecture Repository.

C.  It provides methods for classifying architecture and solution assets.

D.  It is an important aid to communication for architects on both the buy and supply-side.

E.  It is an aid to organization of re-usable and solution assets.

Q2:   Which of the following in the Enterprise Continuum is an example of
      an internal architecture or solution artifact that is available for re-use?
      A.   Deliverables from previous architecture work
      B.   Industry reference models and patterns
      C.   The TOGAF TRM
      D.   The ARTS data model

Q3:   Which of the following in the Enterprise Continuum is *not* an example
      of an external architecture or solution artifact?
      A.   The TOGAF TRM
      B.   IT-specific models, such as web services
      C.   The ARTS data model
      D.   Deliverables from previous architecture work

Q4:   Which of the following best completes the next sentence: The
      Enterprise Continuum aids communication _____
      A.   Within enterprises
      B.   Between enterprises
      C.   With vendor organizations
      D.   By providing a consistent language to communicate the differences
           between architectures
      E.   All of these

Q5:   Which of the following are considered to be the constituent parts of
      the Enterprise Continuum?
      A.   Standards Information Base, Governance Log
      B.   TOGAF TRM, III-RM
      C.   Architecture Continuum, Solutions Continuum
      D.   Business Architecture, Application Architecture

Q6:   Complete the sentence: The TOGAF Integrated Information
      Infrastructure Reference Model (III-RM) is classified in the
      Architecture Continuum as an example of a(n) _____
      A.   Common Systems Architecture
      B.   Industry Architecture
      C.   Enterprise Architecture
      D.   Foundation Architecture

Q7:   Which of the following responses does *not* complete the next sentence? The Solutions Continuum _____

    A.  Provides a way to understand the implementation of assets defined in the Architecture Continuum

    B.  Addresses the commonalities and differences among the products, systems, and services of an implemented system

    C.  Can be considered to have at each level a set of building blocks that represent a solution to the business requirements at that level

    D.  Contains a number of re-usable Architecture Building Blocks

    E.  Has a relationship to the Architecture Continuum that includes guidance, direction, and support

Q8:   Which one of the following reference building blocks is *not* part of the Solutions Continuum?

    A.  Systems libraries

    B.  Organization-specific solutions

    C.  Foundation solutions

    D.  Common systems solutions

    E.  Industry solutions

Q9:   Which of the following is considered a model for a physical instance of the Enterprise Continuum?

    A.  The Architecture Repository

    B.  The III-RM

    C.  The Standards Information Base

    D.  The TOGAF TRM

Q10:  Which class of architectural information held within the Architecture Repository would contain adopted reference models?

    A.  Architecture Metamodel

    B.  Architecture Capability

    C.  Standards Information Base

    D.  Reference Library

Q11:  Which level of the Architecture Landscape contains the most detail?

    A.  Capability Architectures

    B.  Segment Architectures

    C.  Strategic Architectures

Q12:  Which of the following describes a purpose of a Standards Information
      Base?
      A.  To provide a method for architecture development
      B.  To provide a basis for architectural governance
      C.  To provide a record of governance activity
      D.  To show an architectural view of building blocks

## 6.12  Recommended Reading

The following are recommended sources of further information for this
chapter:

*   TOGAF 9 Part V: Enterprise Continuum and Tools (Chapters 38-42)

# Chapter 7

# The ADM Phases

## 7.1 Key Learning Points

This chapter will help you understand how each of the ADM phases contributes to the success of enterprise architecture.

**Key Points Explained**

This chapter will help you to answer the following questions:

- What are the objectives of each of the ADM phases?
- What are the key aspects to the approach taken in each phase for enterprise architecture development?

## 7.2 Preliminary Phase

The Preliminary Phase includes the preparation and initiation activities to create an Architecture Capability. Key activities are as follows:

- Understand the business environment
- Ensure high-level management commitment
- Obtain agreement on scope
- Establish architecture principles
- Establish governance structure
- Customization of TOGAF

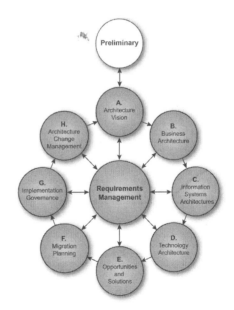

### 7.2.1  Objectives

*(Syllabus Reference: Unit 6, Learning Outcome P.1: You should be able to describe the objectives of the Preliminary Phase.)*

- Determine the Architecture Capability desired by the organization:
  — Review the organizational context for conducting enterprise architecture
  — Identify and scope the elements of the enterprise organizations affected by the Architecture Capability
  — Identify the established frameworks, methods, and processes that intersect with the Architecture Capability
  — Establish a Capability Maturity target
- Establish the Architecture Capability:
  — Define and establish the Organizational Model for Enterprise Architecture
  — Define and establish the detailed process and resources for architecture governance
  — Select and implement tools that support the Architecture Capability
  — Define the architecture principles (see Chapter 8 for more information on architecture principles)

### 7.2.2  Approach

*(Syllabus Reference: Unit 6, Learning Outcome P.2: You should be able to briefly explain the seven aspects of the approach undertaken in the Preliminary Phase.)*

The Preliminary Phase is about defining "where, what, why, who, and how we do architecture" in the enterprise concerned. The main aspects are as follows:

- Defining the enterprise
- Identifying key drivers and elements in the organizational context
- Defining the requirements for architecture work
- Defining the architecture principles that will inform any architecture work
- Defining the framework to be used
- Defining the relationships between management frameworks
- Evaluating the enterprise architecture's maturity

**Defining the Enterprise**

One of the main challenges of enterprise architecture is that of enterprise scope. The scope of the enterprise, and whether it is federated, will determine those stakeholders who will derive most benefit from the new or enhanced enterprise architecture. It is imperative to appoint a sponsor at this stage to ensure that the resultant activity has resources to proceed and the clear support of the business management. The enterprise may include many organizations and the duties of the sponsor are to ensure that all stakeholders are included in defining, establishing, and using the Architecture Capability.

### Identifying Key Drivers and Elements in the Organizational Context

It is necessary to understand the context surrounding the architecture. For example, considerations include:

- The commercial models and budget for the enterprise architecture
- The stakeholders
- The intentions and culture of the organization
- Current processes that support execution of change and operation of the enterprise
- The Baseline Architecture landscape
- The skills and capabilities of the enterprise

Review of the organizational context should provide valuable requirements on how to tailor the architecture framework, particularly the level of formality, the expenditure required, and contact with other organizations.

### Defining the Requirements for Architecture Work

Business imperatives drive the requirements and performance metrics. One or more of the following requirements need to be articulated so that the sponsor can identify the key decision-makers and stakeholders involved in defining and establishing the Architecture Capability:

- Business requirements
- Cultural aspirations
- Organization intents
- Strategic intent
- Forecast financial requirements

Defining the Architecture Principles that will Inform any Architecture Work
The definition of architecture principles is fundamental to the development of an enterprise architecture. Architecture work is informed by business principles as well as architecture principles. The architecture principles themselves are also normally based in part on business principles.

Architecture principles are covered in further detail in Chapter 8.

**Defining the Framework to be Used**

The ADM is a generic method, intended to be used by enterprises in a wide variety of industry types and geographies. It can also be used with a wide variety of other enterprise architecture frameworks, if required. TOGAF has to co-exist with and enhance the operational capabilities of other frameworks in use within an organization. The main frameworks that may need to be coordinated with TOGAF are:

- **Business Capability Management** (Business Direction and Planning) which determine what business capabilities are required.
- **Portfolio/Project Management Methods** which determine how a company manages its change initiatives.
- **Operations Management Methods** which describe how a company runs its day-to-day operations, including IT.
- **Solution Development Methods** which formalize the way that business systems are delivered.

As illustrated in Figure 15, these frameworks are not discrete, and there are significant overlaps between them and the Business Capability Management. Consequently, an enterprise architect must be aware of the impact that the architecture has on the entire enterprise.

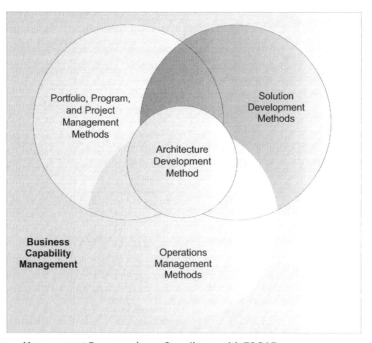

Figure 15:    Management Frameworks to Coordinate with TOGAF

**Defining the Relationships between Management Frameworks**
Figure 16 shows a more detailed set of dependencies between the various
frameworks and business planning activity. The enterprise architecture can be
used to provide a structure for all of the corporate initiatives.

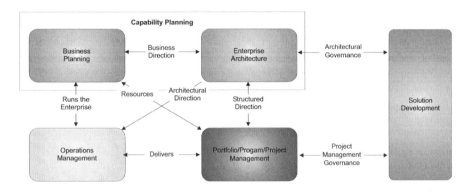

Figure 16:    Interoperability and Relationships between Management Frameworks

The management frameworks are required to complement each other and
work in close harmony for the good of the enterprise.

**Evaluating the Enterprise Architecture Maturity**
Capability Maturity Models (CMMs) are a good way of assessing the ability
of an enterprise to exercise different capabilities. Capability Maturity Models
typically identify selected factors that are required to exercise a capability.
An organization's ability to execute specific factors provides a measure of
maturity and can be used to recommend a series of sequential steps to
improve a capability. It is an assessment that gives executives an insight into
pragmatically improving a capability.

## 7.3  Phase A: Architecture Vision

Phase A is about project
establishment and initiates an
iteration of the Architecture
Development Cycle, setting
the scope, constraints, and
expectations for the iteration.

It is required at the start
of every architecture
cycle in order to create
the Architecture Vision,
validate the business context,
and create the approved
Statement of Architecture
Work.

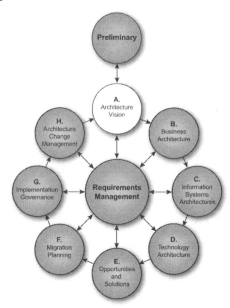

### 7.3.1  Objectives

*(Syllabus Reference: Unit 6, Learning Outcome A.1: You should be able to
describe the main objectives of Phase A.)*

- Develop a high-level aspirational vision of the capabilities and business
  value to be delivered as a result of the proposed enterprise architecture
- Obtain approval for a Statement of Architecture Work that defines a
  program of works to develop and deploy the architecture outlined in the
  Architecture Vision

### 7.3.2  Approach

*(Syllabus Reference: Unit 6, Learning Outcome A.2: You should be able to
briefly explain the two main aspects of the approach for Phase A.)*

Phase A starts with receipt of a Request for Architecture Work from the
sponsoring organization to the architecture organization. A key objective is
to ensure proper recognition and endorsement from corporate management,
and the support and commitment of line management for this evolution of
the ADM cycle.

As the name of the phase suggests, creating the Architecture Vision is a key
activity in this phase. This is discussed below, as is the business scenarios

technique which can be used to develop the Architecture Vision.

**Creating the Architecture Vision**

The Architecture Vision provides the sponsor with a key tool to sell the benefits of the proposed capability to stakeholders and decision-makers within the enterprise. It describes how the new capability will meet the business goals and strategic objectives and address the stakeholder concerns when implemented.

Normally, key elements of the Architecture Vision – such as the enterprise mission, vision, strategy, and goals – have been documented as part of some wider business strategy or enterprise planning activity that has its own lifecycle within the enterprise. In such cases, the activity in Phase A is concerned with verifying and understanding the documented business strategy and goals. Phase A may also integrate the enterprise strategy and goals with the strategy and goals implicit within the current architecture.

In other cases, little or no Business Architecture work may have been done to date. In such cases, there will be a need for the architecture team to research, verify, and gain buy-in to the key business objectives and processes that the architecture is to support. This may be done as a free-standing exercise, either preceding architecture development, or as part of the ADM initiation phase (Preliminary Phase).

Business scenarios (see below) are an appropriate and useful technique to discover and document business requirements, and to articulate an Architecture Vision that responds to those requirements.

The Architecture Vision provides a first-cut, high-level description of the Baseline and Target Architectures, covering the Business, Data, Application, and Technology domains. These outline descriptions are developed in subsequent phases.

Once an Architecture Vision is defined and documented in the Statement of Architecture Work, it is critical to use it to build a consensus. Without this consensus it is very unlikely that the final architecture will be accepted by the organization as a whole. The consensus is represented by the sponsoring organization signing the Statement of Architecture Work.

**Business Scenarios**

The ADM has its own method (a "method-within-a-method") for identifying and articulating the business requirements implied, and the implied architecture requirements. This technique is known as "business scenarios", and is described in detail in Chapter 8. The technique may be used iteratively, at different levels of detail in the hierarchical decomposition of the Business Architecture.

## 7.4 Phase B: Business Architecture

Phase B is about development of a Business Architecture to support an agreed Architecture Vision.

This describes the fundamental organization of a business embodied in:

- Its business process and people
- Their relationships to each other and the people
- The principles governing its design and evolution and shows how an organization meets its business goals.

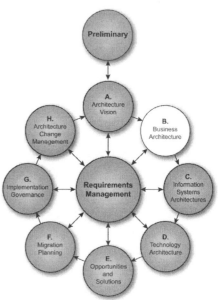

### 7.4.1 Objectives

*(Syllabus Reference: Unit 6, Learning Outcome B.1: You should be able to describe the main objectives of Phase B.)*

- Develop the Target Business Architecture describing how the enterprise needs to operate to achieve the business goals, responds to the strategic drivers set out in the Architecture Vision, and addresses the Request for Architecture Work and stakeholder concerns
- Identify candidate Architecture Roadmap components based upon gaps between the Baseline and Target Business Architectures

## 7.4.2  Approach

*(Syllabus Reference: Unit 6, Learning Outcome B.2: You should be able to explain the main aspects of the approach in Phase B.)*

In summary, the Business Architecture describes the product and/or service strategy, and the organizational, functional, process, information, and geographic aspects of the business environment.

A knowledge of the Business Architecture is a prerequisite for architecture work in any other domain (Data, Application, Technology), and is therefore the first architecture activity that needs to be undertaken.

In practical terms, the Business Architecture is often necessary as a means of demonstrating the business value of subsequent architecture work to key stakeholders, and the return on investment to those stakeholders from supporting and participating in the subsequent work.

**Developing the Baseline Description**

If an enterprise has existing architecture descriptions, they should be used as the basis for the Baseline Description. Where no such descriptions exist, information will have to be gathered in whatever format comes to hand.

The normal approach to Target Architecture development is top-down. In the Baseline Description, however, the analysis of the current state often has to be done bottom-up, particularly where little or no architecture assets exist. In such a case, the architect simply has to document the working assumptions about high-level architectures, and the process is one of gathering evidence to turn the working assumptions into fact.

**Business Modeling**

Business models should be extensions of business scenarios developed during the Architecture Vision. A variety of modeling tools and techniques may be used. Such as **Activity Models** (also called **Business Process Models**), **Use-Case Models**, and **Class Models.** All three types of model can be represented in the Unified Modeling Language (UML), and a variety of tools exist for generating such models. The Defense sector also uses **Node Connectivity Diagrams** and **Information Exchange Matrices**.

**Using the Architecture Repository**

The architecture team will need to consider what relevant Business Architecture resources are available from the Architecture Repository, in particular:

- Generic business models relevant to the organization's industry sector; these are called "Industry Architectures"
- Business models relevant to common high-level business domains (for example, electronic commerce, supply chain management, etc.); these are called "Common Systems Architectures"
- Enterprise-specific building blocks (process components, business rules, job descriptions, etc.)
- Applicable standards

## 7.5  Phase C: Information Systems Architectures

Phase C is about documenting the Information Systems Architectures for an architecture project, including the development of Data and Application Architectures. This describes the major types of information and the application systems that process the information, and their relationships to each other and the environment.

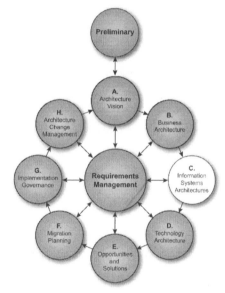

There are two steps in this phase, which may be developed either sequentially or concurrently:

- Data Architecture
- Application Architecture

### 7.5.1  Objectives

*(Syllabus Reference: Unit 6, Learning Outcome C.1: You should be able to describe the main objectives of Phase C.)*

- Develop the Target Information Systems (Data and Application) Architecture, describing how the enterprise's Information Systems Architecture will enable the Business Architecture and the Architecture

Vision, in a way that addresses the Request for Architecture Work and stakeholder concerns.

- Identify candidate Architecture Roadmap components based upon gaps between the Baseline and Target Information Systems (Data and Application) Architectures.

**Consistency of Phases B, C, and D**

As noted in Section 5.2, the architectures developed in Phases B, C, and D follow a uniform step pattern, including development of Baseline and Target Architecture descriptions and analysis of the gaps. The details are out of scope for TOGAF 9 Foundation, and are covered instead in Level 2.

## 7.5.2 Approach

*(Syllabus Reference: Unit 6, Learning Outcome C.2: You should be able to briefly explain the approach recommended by TOGAF for Phase C.)*

Phase C involves some combination of Data and Application Architecture, in either order. Advocates exist for both sequences, and TOGAF leaves this to the user to decide. Consideration of the factors is outside the scope of the TOGAF 9 Foundation Syllabus. The syllabus covers the two topics below.

**Key Considerations for the Data Architecture**

Key considerations for the Data Architecture include:

- **Data Management**

  When an enterprise has chosen to undertake large-scale architectural transformation, it is important to understand and address data management issues. A structured and comprehensive approach to data management enables the effective use of data to capitalize on its competitive advantages.

  Considerations include:

  — Defining application components which will serve as the system of record or reference for enterprise master data

  — Defining enterprise-wide standards that all application components, including software packages, need to adopt

  — Understanding how data entities are utilized by business functions, processes, and services

— Understanding how and where enterprise data entities are created, stored, transported, and reported
— Understanding the level and complexity of data transformations required to support the information exchange needs between applications
— Defining the requirement for software in supporting data integration with the enterprise's customers and suppliers (e.g., use of ETL[10] tools during the data migration, data profiling tools to evaluate data quality, etc.)

- **Data Migration**

When an existing application is replaced, there will be a critical need to migrate data (master, transactional, and reference) to the new application. The Data Architecture should identify data migration requirements and also provide indicators as to the level of transformation, weeding, and cleansing that will be required to present data in a format that meets the requirements and constraints of the target application. The objective is to ensure that the target application has quality data when it is populated. Another key consideration is to ensure that an enterprise-wide common data definition is established to support the transformation.

- **Data Governance**

Considerations for data governance should ensure that the enterprise has the necessary dimensions in place to enable the transformation, as follows:
— Structure: Does the enterprise have the necessary organizational structure and the standards bodies to manage data entity aspects of the transformation?
— Management System: Does the enterprise have the necessary management system and data-related programs to manage the governance aspects of data entities throughout its lifecycle?
— People: What data-related skills and roles does the enterprise require for the transformation? If the enterprise lacks such resources and skills, the enterprise should consider either acquiring those critical skills or training existing internal resources to meet the requirements through a well-defined learning program.

---

10    ETL is an abbreviation for Extract, Transform, and Load.

**Using the Architecture Repository**

As part of this phase, the architecture team should consider what relevant Data Architecture and Application Architecture resources are available in the organization's Architecture Repository; in particular, generic models relevant to the organization's industry "vertical" sector. For example:

- Data Architecture models:
  - ARTS has defined a data model for the Retail industry.
  - Energistics has defined a data model for the Petrotechnical industry.
- Application Architecture models:
  - The TeleManagement Forum (TMF) – www.tmforum.org – has developed detailed applications models relevant to the Telecommunications industry.
  - The Object Management Group (OMG) – www.omg.org – has a number of vertical Domain Task Forces developing software models relevant to specific vertical domains such as Healthcare, Transportation, Finance, etc.
  - Application models relevant to common high-level business functions, such as electronic commerce, supply chain management, etc.

The Open Group has a Reference Model for Integrated Information Infrastructure (III-RM) that focuses on the application-level components and services necessary to provide an integrated information infrastructure.

## 7.6 Phase D: Technology Architecture

Phase D is about documenting the
Technology Architecture for an
architecture project, in the form of the
fundamental organization of the IT
systems:

- Embodied in the hardware,
  software, and communications
  technology
- Their relationships to each other
  and the environment
- The principles governing its design
  and evolution

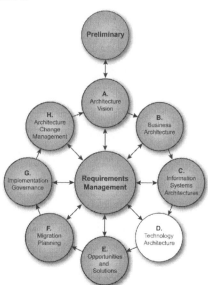

### 7.6.1 Objectives

*(Syllabus Reference: Unit 6, Learning
Outcome D.1: You should be able to describe the main objectives of Phase D.)*

- Develop the Target Technology Architecture that enables the logical and
  physical application and data components and the Architecture Vision,
  addressing the Request for Architecture Work and stakeholder concerns
- Identify candidate Architecture Roadmap components based upon gaps
  between the Baseline and Target Technology Architectures

### 7.6.2 Approach

*(Syllabus Reference: Unit 6, Learning Outcome D.2: You should be able to
briefly explain the approach to Phase D.)*

**Using the Architecture Repository**

As part of Phase D, the architecture team must consider what relevant
Technology Architecture resources are available in the Architecture
Repository. In particular, consider:

- Existing IT services
- The TOGAF Technical Reference Model (TRM)
- Generic technology models relevant to the organization's industry
  "vertical" sector; for example, in the telecommunications industry such
  models have been developed by the TeleManagement Forum (TMF)
- Technology models relevant to Common Systems Architectures; for
  example, the III-RM.

## 7.7 **Phase E: Opportunities and Solutions**

Phase E is the first phase which is directly concerned with implementation. It describes the process of identifying major implementation projects and grouping them into work packages that deliver the Target Architecture identified in previous phases.

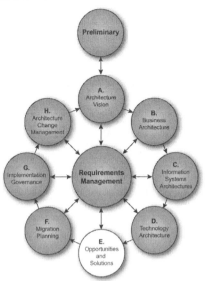

Key activities are as follows:

- Perform initial implementation planning
- Identify the major implementation projects
- Group changes into work packages
- Decide on approach:
  — Make versus buy versus re-use
  — Outsource
  — COTS
  — Open Source
- Assess priorities
- Identify dependencies

### 7.7.1 **Objectives**

*(Syllabus Reference: Unit 6, Learning Outcome E.1: You should be able to describe the main objectives of Phase E.)*

- Generate the initial complete version of the Architecture Roadmap, based upon the gap analysis and candidate Architecture Roadmap components from Phases B, C, and D
- Determine whether an incremental approach is required, and if so identify Transition Architectures that will deliver continuous business value

### 7.7.2 **Approach**

*(Syllabus Reference: Unit 6, Learning Outcome E.2: You should be able to briefly explain the approach to Phase E.)*

Phase E concentrates on how to deliver the architecture. It takes into account the complete set of gaps between the Target and Baseline Architectures in all architecture domains, and logically groups changes into work packages within the enterprise's portfolios. This is an effort to build a best-fit roadmap that is based upon the stakeholder requirements, the enterprise's business transformation readiness, identified opportunities and solutions, and identified implementation constraints. The key is to focus on the final target while realizing incremental business value.

Phase E is the initial step on the creation of a well considered Implementation and Migration Plan that is integrated into the enterprise's portfolio in Phase F.

There are four key concepts in the transition from developing to delivering a Target Architecture:
- Architecture Roadmap
- Work Packages
- Transition Architectures
- Implementation and Migration Plan

The Architecture Roadmap lists individual work packages in a timeline that will realize the Target Architecture. Each work package identifies a logical group of changes necessary to realize the Target Architecture. A Transition Architecture describes the enterprise at an architecturally significant state between the Baseline and Target Architectures. Transition Architectures provide interim Target Architectures upon which the organization can converge. The Implementation and Migration Plan provides a schedule of the projects that will realize the Target Architecture.

## 7.8  Phase F: Migration Planning

Phase F addresses detailed
migration planning; that
is, how to move from the
Baseline to the Target
Architectures.

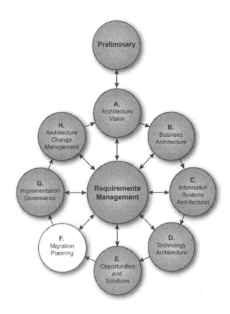

Key activities include:
- For work packages
  and projects identified,
  perform a cost/benefit
  analysis and a risk
  assessment
- Finalize a detailed
  Implementation and
  Migration Plan

### 7.8.1  Objectives

*(Syllabus Reference: Unit 6, Learning Outcome F.1: You should be able to
describe the main objectives for Phase F.)*
- Finalize the Architecture Roadmap and the supporting Implementation
  and Migration Plan
- Ensure that the Implementation and Migration Plan is coordinated with
  the enterprise's approach to managing and implementing change in the
  enterprise's overall change portfolio
- Ensure that the business value and cost of work packages and Transition
  Architectures is understood by key stakeholders

### 7.8.2  Approach

*(Syllabus Reference: Unit 6, Learning Outcome F.2: You should be able to briefly
explain the approach to Phase F.)*

The focus of Phase F is the creation of an Implementation and Migration
Plan in co-operation with the portfolio and project managers. Phase E
provides an incomplete Architecture Roadmap and Implementation and
Migration Plan that address the Request for Architecture Work. In Phase F
this Roadmap and the Implementation and Migration Plan are integrated
with the enterprise's other change activity. Activities include assessing the
dependencies, costs, and benefits of the various migration projects. The

Architecture Roadmap, and Implementation and Migration Plan, from Phase E will form the basis of the detailed Implementation and Migration Plan that will include portfolio and project-level detail. The architecture development cycle should then be completed, and lessons learned documented to enable continuous process improvement.

## 7.9 Phase G: Implementation Governance

Phase G defines how the architecture constrains the implementation projects, monitors it while building it, and produces a signed Architecture Contract.

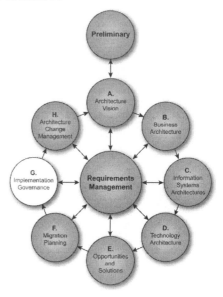

Key activities include:

- Provide architectural oversight for the implementation
- Define architecture constraints on implementation projects
- Govern and manage an Architecture Contract
- Monitor implementation work for conformance

### 7.9.1 Objectives

*(Syllabus Reference: Unit 6, Learning Outcome G.1: You should be able to describe the main objectives of Phase G.)*

- Ensure conformance with the Target Architecture by implementation projects
- Perform appropriate Architecture Governance functions for the solution and any implementation-driven architecture Change Requests

### 7.9.2 Approach

*(Syllabus Reference: Unit 6, Learning Outcome G.2: You should be able to briefly explain the approach to Phase G.)*

In Phase G all the information for successful management of the various implementation projects is brought together. The actual development occurs in parallel with Phase G.

The approach in Phase G is to:
- Establish an implementation program that will enable the delivery of the agreed Transition Architectures
- Adopt a phased deployment schedule that reflects the business priorities embodied in the Architecture Roadmap
- Follow the organization's standard for corporate, IT, and Architecture Governance
- Use the organization's established portfolio/program management approach, where this exists
- Define an operations framework to ensure the effective long life of the deployed solution

A key aspect of Phase G is ensuring compliance with the defined architecture(s), not only by the implementation projects, but also by other ongoing projects.

## 7.10  Phase H: Architecture Change Management

Phase H ensures that changes to the architecture are managed in a controlled manner.

Key activities include:
- Provide continual monitoring and a change management process
- Ensure that changes to the architecture are managed in a cohesive and architected way
- Provide flexibility to evolve rapidly in response to changes in the technology or business environment
- Monitor the business and capacity management

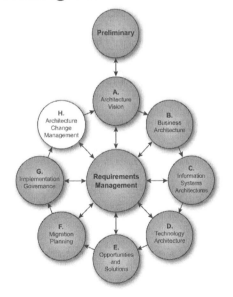

### 7.10.1  Objectives

*(Syllabus Reference: Unit 6, Learning Outcome H.1: You should be able to describe the main objectives of Phase G.)*

- Ensure that the architecture lifecycle is maintained
- Ensure that the Architecture Governance Framework is executed
- Ensure that the enterprise's Architecture Capability meets current requirements

### 7.10.2  Approach

*(Syllabus Reference: Unit 6, Learning Outcome H.2: You should be able to briefly explain the approach to Phase H.)*

The goal of an architecture change management process is to ensure that the architecture achieves its original target business value. Monitoring business growth and decline is a critical aspect of this phase.

The value and change management process, once established, will determine:

- The circumstances under which the enterprise architecture, or parts of it, will be permitted to change after deployment, and the process by which that will happen
- The circumstances under which the Architecture Development Cycle will be initiated to develop a new architecture

**Drivers for Change**

There are three ways to change the existing infrastructure that have to be integrated:

1. Strategic, top-down directed change to enhance or create new capability (capital)
2. Bottom-up changes to correct or enhance capability (operations and maintenance) for infrastructure under operations management
3. Experiences with the previously delivered project increments in the care of operations management, but still being delivered by ongoing projects

**Enterprise Architecture Change Management Process**

The enterprise architecture change management process needs to determine how changes are to be managed, what techniques are to be applied, and what methodologies used.

TOGAF recommends the following approach based on classifying the required architectural changes into one of three categories:

- **Simplification change**: A simplification change can normally be handled via change management techniques.

- **Incremental change**: An incremental change may be capable of being handled via change management techniques, or it may require partial re-architecting, depending on the nature of the change (see Guidelines for Maintenance versus Architecture Redesign for guidance).
- **Re-architecting change**: A re-architecting change requires putting the whole architecture through the Architecture Development Cycle again.

Another way of looking at these three choices is as follows:
- A simplification change to an architecture is often driven by a requirement to reduce investment.
- An incremental change is driven by a requirement to derive additional value from existing investment.
- A re-architecting change is driven by a requirement to increase investment in order to create new value for exploitation.

To determine whether a change is simplification, incremental, or re-architecting, the following activities are undertaken:
1. Registration of all events that may impact the architecture
2. Resource allocation and management for architecture tasks
3. The process or role responsible for architecture resources has to make an assessment of what should be done
4. Evaluation of impacts

**Guidelines for Maintenance versus Architecture Redesign**
A good rule-of-thumb is:
- If the change impacts two stakeholders or more, then it is likely to require an architecture redesign and re-entry to the ADM.
- If the change impacts only one stakeholder, then it is more likely to be a candidate for change management.
- If the change can be allowed under a dispensation, then it is more likely to be a candidate for change management.

For example:
- If the impact is significant for the business strategy, then there may be a need to re-do the whole enterprise architecture – thus a re-architecting approach.

- If a new technology or a standard emerges, then there may be a need to refresh the Technology Architecture, but not the whole enterprise architecture – thus an incremental change.
- If the change is at an infrastructure level – for example, ten systems reduced or changed to one system – this may not change the architecture above the physical layer, but it will change the Baseline Description of the Technology Architecture. This would be a simplification change handled via change management techniques.

In particular, a refreshment cycle (partial or complete re-architecting) may be required if:
- The Foundation Architecture needs to be re-aligned with the business strategy.
- Substantial change is required to components and guidelines for use in deployment of the architecture.
- Significant standards used in the product architecture are changed which have significant end-user impact; e.g., regulatory changes.

If there is a need for a refreshment cycle, then a new Request for Architecture Work must be issued (to move to another cycle).

## 7.11  Requirements Management

*(Syllabus Reference: Unit 6, Learning Outcome R.1: You should be able to briefly explain how Requirements Management fits into the ADM cycle.)*

The process of managing architecture requirements applies to all phases of the ADM cycle. The Requirements Management process is a dynamic process, which addresses the identification of requirements for the enterprise, stores them, and then feeds them in and out of the relevant ADM phases.

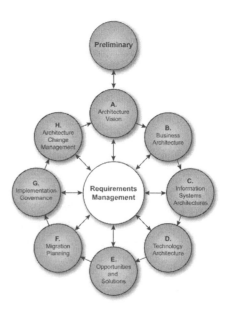

As shown by its central placement in the ADM cycle diagram, this process is central to driving the ADM process.

### 7.11.1 Objectives

*(Syllabus Reference: Unit 6, Learning Outcome R.2: You should be able to describe the nature of the Requirements Management process.)*

- Ensure that the Requirements Management process is sustained and operates for all relevant ADM phases
- Manage architecture requirements identified during any execution of the ADM cycle or a phase
- Ensure that the relevant architecture requirements are available for use by each phase as the phase is executed

### 7.11.2 Approach

*(Syllabus Reference: Unit 6, Learning Outcome R.3: You should be able to describe the approach to Requirements Management.)*

The ADM is continuously driven by the Requirements Management process. The ability to deal with changes in requirements is crucial, as architecture by its nature deals with uncertainty and change, bridging the divide between the aspirations of the stakeholders and what can be delivered as a practical solution.

**Requirements Management Manages the Flow of Requirements**

Note that the Requirements Management process itself does not dispose of, address, or prioritize any requirements; this is done within the relevant phase of the ADM.

It is recommended that a Requirements Repository is used to record and manage all architecture requirements. TOGAF does not mandate or recommend any specific process or tool for requirements management; it simply states what an effective Requirements Management process should achieve, which could be thought of as "the requirements for requirements".

TOGAF suggests a number of resources in this area:

**Business Scenarios**

Business scenarios are an appropriate and useful technique to discover and document business requirements, and to describe an Architecture Vision that responds to those requirements. Business scenarios are described in detail in TOGAF 9 Part III: ADM Guidelines and Techniques, Chapter 26 (Business Scenarios).

**Other Requirements Tools**

There is a large and increasing, number of Commercial Off-The-Shelf (COTS) tools available for the support of requirements management. The Volere web site has a useful list of requirements tools (see www.volere.co.uk/tools.htm).

## 7.12 Summary

This chapter has described each of the ADM phases and how they contribute to the development of an enterprise architecture. This has included the key objectives for each phase, together with high-level considerations for the approach.

## 7.13 Test Yourself Questions

Q1:  Which of the ADM phases includes the development of Application and Data Architectures?
   A.   Phase A
   B.   Phase B
   C.   Phase C
   D.   Phase D
   E.   Phase E

Q2:  Which of the ADM phases includes the objective of establishing the organizational model for enterprise architecture?
   A.   Preliminary
   B.   Phase A
   C.   Phase B
   D.   Phase D
   E.   Phase E

Q3:   Which one of the following is an objective of Phase A?
A.   To review the stakeholders, their requirements, and priorities
B.   To develop a high-level vision of the business value to be delivered
C.   To generate and gain consensus on an outline Implementation and Migration Strategy
D.   To formulate recommendations for each implementation project
E.   To provide a process to manage architecture requirements

Q4:   Complete the sentence: According to TOGAF, all of the following are part of the approach to the Preliminary Phase, except _____
A.   Creating the Architecture Vision
B.   Defining the enterprise
C.   Defining the framework to be used
D.   Defining the relationships between management frameworks
E.   Evaluating the enterprise architecture maturity

Q5:   Which one of the following is a recommended way to evaluate the enterprise architecture maturity?
A.   Architecture Principles
B.   Business Scenarios
C.   Capability Maturity Models
D.   Risk Management

Q6:   Which of the ADM phases commences with receipt of a Request for Architecture Work from the sponsor?
A.   Preliminary
B.   Phase A
C.   Phase E
D.   Phase G
E.   Phase H

Q7:   Which of the following is a technique that can be used to discover and document business requirements in Phase A?
A.   Business Scenarios
B.   Business Transformation Readiness Assessment
C.   Gap Analysis
D.   Stakeholder Management

Q8:   Which architecture domain is the first architecture activity undertaken
      in the ADM cycle?
      A.   Application
      B.   Business
      C.   Data
      D.   Technology

Q9:   Which one of the following is considered a relevant resource for Phase
      B available from the Architecture Repository?
      A.   The ARTS data model
      B.   Business rules, job descriptions
      C.   The III-RM
      D.   The TOGAF Technical Reference Model

Q10:  Which one of the following is a potential resource in Phase C and
      is a reference model focusing on application-level components and
      services?
      A.   The ARTS data model
      B.   Business rules, job descriptions
      C.   The III-RM
      D.   The TOGAF Technical Reference Model

Q11:  In which ADM phase is an outline Implementation and Migration
      Strategy generated?
      A.   Phase E
      B.   Phase F
      C.   Phase G
      D.   Phase H

Q12:  In which ADM phase are the Transition Architectures defined in Phase
      E confirmed with the stakeholders?
      A.   Phase E
      B.   Phase F
      C.   Phase G
      D.   Phase H

Q13: In which ADM phase is an Architecture Contract developed to cover the overall implementation and deployment process?
    A.   Phase E
    B.   Phase F
    C.   Phase G
    D.   Phase H

Q14: Which one of the following is an objective of Phase H: Architecture Change Management?
    A.   Finalize the Architecture Roadmap
    B.   Manage architecture requirements identified during execution of the ADM cycle
    C.   Perform Architecture Governance functions for the solution
    D.   Operate the Architecture Governance Framework

Q15: Which one of the following is a change that can always be handled by change management techniques?
    A.   Incremental change
    B.   Re-architecting change
    C.   Simplification change

Q16: Complete the sentence: The process of managing architecture requirements applies to _____?
    A.   All ADM phases
    B.   The Preliminary Phase
    C.   Phase A: Architecture Vision
    D.   The Requirements Management phase

## 7.14 Recommended Reading

The following are recommended sources of further information for this chapter:

- TOGAF 9 Part II: ADM, Chapters 6 through 17, Phases Preliminary to Phase H, and Requirements Management

# Chapter 8

# ADM Guidelines and Techniques

## 8.1 Key Learning Points

This chapter will help you understand the guidelines and techniques provided to support application of the Architecture Development Method (ADM).

**Key Points Explained**

This chapter will help you to answer the following questions:

- What are the contents of Part III of TOGAF 9?
- What is an architecture principle?
- Why are architecture principles needed and where are they used within TOGAF?
- What is a business scenario?
- What is the gap analysis technique?
- What does TOGAF mean by interoperability?
- What is Business Transformation Readiness?
- What are the main characteristics of Risk Management?
- What is Capability-Based Planning?

## 8.2 ADM Guidelines and Techniques Overview

*(Syllabus Reference: Unit 7, Learning Outcome 1: You should be able to briefly explain the contents of Part III of TOGAF 9.)*

TOGAF 9 Part III: ADM Guidelines and Techniques contains a collection of guidelines and techniques for use in applying TOGAF and the ADM. The guidelines document how to adapt the ADM process, whereas the techniques are used when applying the ADM process.

Guidelines for adapting the ADM process include:

- Ways to apply iteration to the ADM
- Applying the ADM at different levels of the enterprise
- Security considerations when applying the ADM
- Using TOGAF to define Service-Oriented Architectures (SOAs)

**TOGAF 9 Foundation Syllabus Coverage**

The TOGAF 9 Foundation Syllabus covers the following subset of the materials in
TOGAF 9 Part III:

- Architecture Principles
- Stakeholder Management
- Architecture Patterns
- Business Scenarios
- Gap Analysis
- Migration Planning Techniques
- Interoperability Requirements
- Business Transformation Readiness Assessment
- Risk Management
- Capability-Based Planning

## 8.3  Architecture Principles

*(Syllabus Reference: Unit 7, Learning Outcome 2: You should be able to briefly
explain the need for architecture principles and where they are used within
TOGAF.)*

Architecture principles are a set of general rules and guidelines for the
architecture being developed.

They are intended to be enduring and seldom amended, and inform and
support the way in which an organization sets about fulfilling its mission.
Often they are one element of a structured set of ideas that collectively define
and guide the organization, from values through to actions and results.

Principles are an initial output of the Preliminary Phase and are used
throughout the ADM to provide a framework for guiding decision-making
within the enterprise.

Depending on the organization, principles may be established within
different domains and at different levels. Two key domains inform the
development and utilization of architecture:
- **Enterprise principles** provide a basis for decision-making throughout
  an enterprise and dictate how the organization fulfills its mission. Such

principles are commonly used as a means of harmonizing decision-making. They are a key element in a successful Architecture Governance strategy. Within the broad domain of enterprise principles, it is common to have subsidiary principles within a business or organizational unit; for example IT, HR, domestic operations, or overseas operations.

- **Architecture principles** are a set of principles that relate to architecture work. They reflect consensus across the enterprise, and embody the spirit of the enterprise architecture. Architecture principles govern the architecture process, affecting the development, maintenance, and use of the enterprise architecture.

> TOGAF 9 Part III: ADM Guidelines and Techniques contains guidelines for developing principles and a detailed set of generic architecture principles.

### 8.3.1  The TOGAF Template for Defining Architecture Principles

*(Syllabus Reference: Unit 7, Learning Outcome 3: You should be able to describe the standard template for architecture principles.)*

TOGAF defines a standard way of describing principles, as shown in Table 9. In addition to a definition statement, each principle should have associated rationale and implication statements, both to promote understanding and acceptance of the principles themselves, and to support the use of the principles in explaining and justifying why specific decisions are made.

Table 9:   TOGAF Template for Defining Principles

| Section | Description |
|---|---|
| **Name** | Should represent both the essence of the rule and be easy to remember. Specific technology platforms should not be mentioned in the name or statement of a principle. Avoid ambiguous words in the name and in the statement such as: "support", "open", "consider", and for lack of good measure the word "avoid", itself, be careful with "manage(ment)", and look for unnecessary adjectives and adverbs. |
| **Statement** | Should succinctly and unambiguously communicate the fundamental rule. For the most part, the principle's statements for managing information are similar among organizations. It is vital that the statement be unambiguous. |

| Section | Description |
|---|---|
| **Rationale** | Should highlight the business benefits of adhering to the principle, using business terminology. Point to the similarity of information and technology principles to the principles governing business operations. Also describe the relationship to other principles, and the intentions regarding a balanced interpretation. Describe situations where one principle would be given precedence or carry more weight than another for making a decision. |
| **Implications** | Should highlight the requirements, both for the business and IT, for carrying out the principle – in terms of resources, costs, and activities/tasks. It will often be apparent that current systems, standards, or practices would be incongruent with the principle upon adoption. The impact on the business and consequences of adopting a principle should be clearly stated. The reader should readily discern the answer to: "How does this affect me?" It is important not to oversimplify, trivialize, or judge the merit of the impact. Some of the implications will be identified as potential impacts only, and may be speculative rather than fully analyzed. |

Example 1:   Simple Principle

| **Self-Serve** | |
|---|---|
| Statement | Customers should be able to serve themselves. |
| Rationale | Applying this principle will improve customer satisfaction, reduce administrative overhead, and potentially improve revenue. |
| Implications | There is an implication to improve ease-of-use and minimize training needs; for example, members should be able to update their contact details, etc. and be able to buy additional membership products online. |

## 8.3.2   What Makes a Good Architecture Principle?

*(Syllabus Reference: Unit 7, Learning Outcome 4: You should be able to explain what makes a good architecture principle.)*

There are five criteria that distinguish a good set of principles, as shown in Table 10.

Table 10:    Recommended Criteria for Quality Principles

| Criteria | Description |
|---|---|
| **Understandability** | The underlying tenets of a principle can be quickly grasped and understood by individuals throughout the organization. The intention of the principle is clear and unambiguous, so that violations, whether intentional or not, are minimized. |
| **Robustness** | Principles should enable good quality decisions about architectures and plans to be made, and enforceable policies and standards to be created. Each principle should be sufficiently definitive and precise to support consistent decision-making in complex, potentially controversial situations. |
| **Completeness** | Every potentially important principle governing the management of information and technology for the organization is defined. The principles cover every situation perceived. |
| **Consistency** | Strict adherence to one principle may require a loose interpretation of another principle. The set of principles must be expressed in a way that allows a balance of interpretations. Principles should not be contradictory to the point where adhering to one principle would violate the spirit of another. Every word in a principle statement should be carefully chosen to allow consistent yet flexible interpretation. |
| **Stability** | Principles should be enduring, yet able to accommodate changes. An amendment process should be established for adding, removing, or altering principles after they are ratified initially. |

## 8.4  Business Scenarios

### 8.4.1  What is a Business Scenario?

*(Syllabus Reference: Unit 7, Learning Outcome 5: You should understand what a business scenario is and its purpose.)*

A key factor in the success of any other major project is the extent to which it is linked to business requirements, and demonstrably supports and enables the enterprise to achieve its business objectives. Business scenarios are a technique used to help identify and understand the business requirements that an architecture must address.

A business scenario describes:
- A business process, application, or set of applications
- The business and technology environment

- The people and computing components ("actors") who execute the scenario
- The desired outcome of proper execution

The technique may be used iteratively, at different levels of detail in the hierarchical decomposition of the Business Architecture. The generic business scenario process is as follows:

1. Identify, document, and rank the problem that is driving the project
2. Document, as high-level architecture models, the business and technical environments where the problem situation is occurring
3. Identify and document desired objectives; the results of handling the problems successfully
4. Identify human actors and their place in the business model, the human participants, and their roles
5. Identify computer actors and their place in the technology model, the computing elements, and their roles
6. Identify and document roles, responsibilities, and measures of success per actor, the required scripts per actor, and the desired results of handling the situation properly
7. Check for fitness-for-purpose of inspiring subsequent architecture work, and refine only if necessary

This is also summarized in Figure 17.

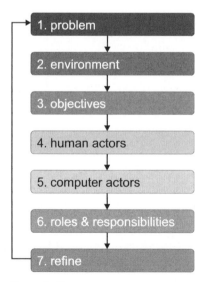

Figure 17:   The Business Scenario Process

A good business scenario represents a significant business need or problem, and enables vendors to understand the value of a solution to the customer. A good business scenario is also "SMART":

- Specific, by defining what needs to be done
- Measurable, through clear metrics for success
- Actionable, by clearly segmenting the problem and providing the basis for a solution
- Realistic, in that the problem can be solved within the bounds of physical reality, time, and cost constraints
- Time-bound, in that there is a clear statement of when the opportunity expires

### 8.4.2  The Use of Business Scenarios in the ADM

*(Syllabus Reference: Unit 7, Learning Outcome 6: You should be able to explain where business scenarios are used within the ADM cycle.)*

Business scenarios figure most prominently in the initial phase of an ADM cycle, Architecture Vision, when they are used to define relevant business requirements, and to build consensus with business management and other stakeholders.

They may also be used in other phases, particularly during Business Architecture, to derive the characteristics of the architecture directly from the high-level requirements of the business.

Because business requirements are important throughout all phases of the ADM cycle, the business scenario technique has an important role to play in the TOGAF ADM, by ensuring that the business requirements themselves are complete and correct.

## 8.5  Gap Analysis

*(Syllabus Reference: Unit 7, Learning Outcome 7: You should be able to explain the purpose of gap analysis.)*

The technique known as gap analysis is widely used in the ADM to validate an architecture that is being developed. A key step in validating an architecture is to consider what may have been forgotten. The architecture must support all of the essential information processing needs of the organization. The most critical source of gaps that should be considered is stakeholder concerns that have not been addressed in prior architectural work.

The basic premise is to highlight a shortfall between the Baseline Architecture and the Target Architecture; that is, items that have been deliberately omitted, accidentally left out, or not yet defined.

Potential sources of gaps include:

- Business domain gaps:
  — People gaps (e.g., cross-training requirements)
  — Process gaps (e.g., process inefficiencies)
  — Tools gaps (e.g., duplicate or missing tool functionality)
  — Information gaps
  — Measurement gaps
  — Financial gaps
  — Facilities gaps (buildings, office space, etc.)
- Data domain gaps:
  — Data not of sufficient currency
  — Data not located where it is needed
  — Not the data that is needed
  — Data not available when needed
  — Data not created
  — Data not consumed
  — Data relationship gaps
- Applications impacted, eliminated, or created
- Technologies impacted, eliminated, or created

*(Syllabus Reference: Unit 7, Learning Outcome 8: You should be able to describe the gap analysis technique.)*

The steps are as follows:

- Draw up a matrix with all the Architecture Building Blocks (ABBs) of the Baseline Architecture on the vertical axis, and all the ABBs of the Target Architecture on the horizontal axis.
- Add to the Baseline Architecture axis a final row labeled "New ABBs", and to the Target Architecture axis a final column labeled "Eliminated ABBs".
- Where an ABB is available in both the Baseline and Target Architectures, record this with "Included" at the intersecting cell.
- Where an ABB from the Baseline Architecture is missing in the Target Architecture, each must be reviewed. If it was correctly eliminated,

mark it as such in the appropriate "Eliminated" cell. If it was not, you have uncovered an accidental omission in your Target Architecture that must be addressed by reinstating the ABB in the next iteration of the architecture design – mark it as such in the appropriate "Eliminated" cell.

*   Where an ABB from the Target Architecture cannot be found in the Baseline Architecture, mark it at the intersection with the "New" row as a gap that needs to filled, either by developing or procuring the building block.

When the exercise is complete, anything under "Eliminated Services" or "New Services" is a gap, which should either be explained as correctly eliminated, or marked as to be addressed by reinstating or developing/procuring the function.

Table 11 shows examples of gaps between the Baseline Architecture and the Target Architecture; in this case the missing elements are "broadcast services" and "shared screen services".

Table 11:   Gap Analysis Example

| Target Architecture → Baseline Architecture ↓ | Video Conferencing Services | Enhanced Telephony Services | Mailing List Services | Eliminated Services ↓ |
|---|---|---|---|---|
| Broadcast Services | | | | Intentionally Eliminated |
| Video Conferencing Services | Included | | | |
| Enhanced Telephony Services | | Potential Match | | |
| Shared Screen Services | | | | Unintentionally excluded – a gap in Target Architecture |
| New → | | Gap: Enhanced services to be developed or produced | Gap: Enhanced services to be developed or produced | |

The gap analysis technique should be used in Phases B, C, D, and E of the ADM.

## 8.6  Interoperability

*(Syllabus Reference: Unit 7, Learning Outcome 9: You should be able to explain the term interoperability.)*

TOGAF defines interoperability as "the ability to share information and services". Defining the degree to which information and services are to be shared is very important, especially in a complex organization and/or extended enterprise.

Many organizations find it useful to categorize interoperability as follows:

- **Operational or Business Interoperability** defines how business processes are to be shared.
- **Information Interoperability** defines how information is to be shared.
- **Technical Interoperability** defines how technical services are to be shared or at least connect to one another.

From an IT perspective, it is also useful to consider interoperability in a similar vein to Enterprise Application Integration (EAI); specifically:

- **Presentation Integration/Interoperability** is where a common look-and-feel approach through a common portal-like solution guides the user to the underlying functionality of the set of systems.
- **Information Integration/Interoperability** is where the corporate information is seamlessly shared between the various corporate applications to achieve, for example, a common set of client information. Normally this is based upon a commonly accepted corporate ontology and shared services for the structure, quality, access, and security/privacy for the information.
- **Application Integration/Interoperability** is where the corporate functionality is integrated and shareable so that the applications are not duplicated (e.g., one change of address service/component; not one for every application) and are seamlessly linked together through functionality such as workflow. This impacts the business and infrastructure applications and is very closely linked to corporate business process unification/interoperability.

- **Technical Integration/Interoperability** includes common methods and shared services for the communication, storage, processing, and access to data primarily in the application platform and communications infrastructure domains. This interoperability is premised upon the degree of rationalization of the corporate IT infrastructure, based upon standards and/or common IT platforms. For example, multiple applications sharing one infrastructure or 10,000 corporate web sites using one centralized content management/web server (rather than thousands of servers and webmasters spread throughout the country/globe).

Example 2:    Example Interoperability Model

**Example Interoperability Model**

An example interoperability model from the Canadian Government follows. This model includes a high-level definition of three classes of interoperability and the nature of the information and services shared at each level. Interoperability is coined in terms of e-enablers for e-Government. The interoperability breakdown is as follows:

- Information interoperability:
    - Knowledge management
    - Business intelligence
    - Information management
    - Trusted identity
- Business interoperability:
    - Delivery networks
    - e-Democracy
    - e-Business
    - Enterprise resource management
    - Relationship and case management
- Technical interoperability:
    - IT infrastructure

### 8.6.1  Interoperability and the ADM

*(Syllabus Reference: Unit 7, Learning Outcome 10: You should understand where interoperability requirements are used within the ADM.)*

The determination of interoperability occurs throughout the ADM:

- In Phase A: Architecture Vision, the nature and security considerations of information and service exchanges are found using business scenarios.

- In Phase B: Business Architecture, information and service exchanges are defined in business terms.
- In Phase C: Data Architecture, the content of information exchanges is detailed using the corporate data and/or information exchange model.
- In Phase C: Application Architecture, the ways that applications are to share information and services are specified.
- In Phase D: Technology Architecture, appropriate technical mechanisms to permit information and service exchanges are specified.
- In Phase E: Opportunities & Solutions, actual solutions are selected.
- In Phase F: Migration Planning, interoperability is implemented logically.

## 8.7 Business Transformation Readiness Assessment

*(Syllabus Reference: Unit 7, Learning Outcome 11: You should understand Business Transformation Readiness Assessment.)*

Enterprise architecture often involves considerable change. Business Transformation Readiness Assessment provides a technique for understanding the readiness of an organization to accept change, identifying the issues, and dealing with them in the Implementation and Migration Plan. It is based on the Canadian Government Business Transformation Enablement Program (BTEP).

*(Syllabus Reference: Unit 7, Learning Outcome 12: You should understand where the Business Transformation Readiness Assessment technique is used within the ADM.)*

Use of such a technique is key to a successful architecture transformation in Phases E and F. An initial assessment of business transformation readiness is carried out in Phase A.

This assessment is recommended to be a joint effort between corporate staff, lines of business, and IT planners.

The recommended activities are:

- Determine the readiness factors that will impact the organization
- Present the readiness factors using maturity models
- Assess the readiness factors, and determine the readiness factor ratings

- Assess the risks for each readiness factor and identify improvement actions to mitigate the risk
- Document the findings into the Capability Assessment and later incorporate the actions into the Implementation and Migration Plan in Phases E and F

## 8.8 Risk Management

*(Syllabus Reference: Unit 7, Learning Outcome 13: You should understand the characteristics of Risk Management.)*

Risk management, documented in TOGAF 9 Part III: ADM Guidelines and Techniques, Chapter 31 (Risk Management), is a technique used to mitigate risk when implementing an architecture project. There are two levels of risk that should be considered:

1. Initial Level of Risk: Risk categorization prior to determining and implementing mitigating actions.
2. Residual Level of Risk: Risk categorization after implementation of mitigating actions.

The recommended process for managing risk consists of the following activities:
- Risk classification
- Risk identification
- Initial risk assessment
- Risk mitigation and residual risk assessment
- Risk monitoring

### 8.8.1 Risk Management in the ADM

*(Syllabus Reference: Unit 7, Learning Outcome 14: You should understand where risk management is used within the TOGAF ADM.)*

Risk is pervasive in any enterprise architecture activity and present in all phases within the ADM. Identification of business transformation risks and mitigation activities is first determined in Phase A as part of the initial Business Transformation Readiness Assessment. It is recommended that risk mitigation activities be included within the Statement of Architecture Work.

The risk identification and mitigation assessment worksheets are maintained as governance artifacts and are kept up-to-date in Phase G (Implementation Governance) where risk monitoring is conducted.

Implementation governance can identify critical risks that are not being mitigated and might require another full or partial ADM cycle.

## 8.9 Capability-Based Planning

*(Syllabus Reference: Unit 7, Learning Outcome 15: You should understand Capability-Based Planning.)*

Capability-Based Planning is a business planning technique that focuses on business outcomes. It is business-driven and business-led and combines the requisite efforts of all lines of business to achieve the desired capability. It accommodates most, if not all, of the corporate business models and is especially useful in organizations where a latent capability to respond (e.g., an emergency preparedness unit) is required and the same resources are involved in multiple capabilities. Often the need for these capabilities is discovered and refined using business scenarios.

Figure 18 illustrates the relationship between Capability-Based Planning, enterprise architecture, and portfolio/project management.

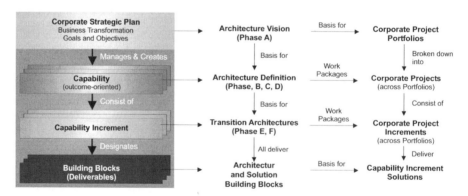

Figure 18: Relationship between Capabilities, Enterprise Architecture, and Projects

## 8.10  Summary

This chapter has introduced a number of key guidelines and techniques that are used to support application of the ADM. This has included:

- Understanding the contents of Part III of TOGAF 9
- The use of architecture principles, including what they are and why they are needed
- The business scenario technique, including what it is and where it is used in the ADM
- The gap analysis technique and its purpose
- The term interoperability, categorizations of interoperability, and where interoperability requirements are used within the ADM
- The Business Transformation Readiness Assessment technique, including what it is and where it is used in the ADM
- The main characteristics of risk management, and where it is used in the ADM
- Capability-Based Planning

## 8.11  Test Yourself Questions

Q1:   Which one of the following statements about architecture principles is not true?

    A.   They are a set of general rules for the architecture being developed.

    B.   They are intended to be enduring and seldom amended.

    C.   They are an initial output from the Preliminary Phase.

    D.   They are used in the Requirements Management phase to dispose of, address, and prioritize requirements.

Q2:   Which part of the TOGAF template for defining architecture principles should highlight the business benefits of adhering to the principle?

    A.   Implications

    B.   Name

    C.   Rationale

    D.   Statement

Q3:    According to TOGAF, a good business scenario should be "SMART".
       What does the letter "S" stand for?
       A.   Solution-oriented
       B.   Specific
       C.   Strategic
       D.   Stakeholder-oriented
       E.   Segmented

Q4:    Where is the business scenario technique most prominently used in
       the ADM cycle?
       A.   Preliminary Phase
       B.   Phase A: Architecture Vision
       C.   Phase F: Migration Planning
       D.   Phase H: Architecture Change Management

Q5.    When performing gap analysis, which of the following is not a valid
       response to the case of an Architecture Building Block that was
       present in the Baseline Architecture found to be missing in the Target
       Architecture?
       A.   A review should occur.
       B.   If the building block was correctly eliminated, it should be added
            to the Target Architecture in the next iteration.
       C.   If the building block was correctly eliminated, it should marked as
            such in the "Eliminated" cell.
       D.   If the building block was incorrectly eliminated, it should be
            reinstated to the architecture design in the next iteration.
       E.   If the building block was incorrectly eliminated, it should be
            recorded as an accidental omission.

Q6.    TOGAF defines interoperability as "the ability to share information
       and services". Which of the following categories utilizes a common
       look-and-feel approach through a common portal-like solution to
       interact with the users?
       A.   Application interoperability
       B.   Information interoperability
       C.   Presentation interoperability
       D.   Technical interoperability

Q7.  Which of the following best describes the Business Transformation
     Readiness Assessment technique?
     A.  A technique to define the degree to which information and
         services are to be shared
     B.  A technique used to validate an architecture
     C.  A technique used to identify and understand the business
         requirements an architecture must address
     D.  A technique used to develop general rules and guidelines for the
         architecture being developed
     E.  A technique used to understand the readiness of an organization
         to accept change

Q8.  Which of the following best describes the meaning of "Residual Level
     of Risk" in risk management?
     A.  The categorization prior to determining risks
     B.  The categorization after implementing mitigating actions
     C.  The categorization after the initial risk assessment
     D.  The categorization after risk identification

Q9.  Which of the following best describes the Capability-Based Planning
     technique?
     A.  A technique used to plan the degree to which information and
         services are to be shared
     B.  A technique used to validate an architecture
     C.  A technique used for business planning that focuses on business
         outcomes
     D.  A technique used to develop general rules and guidelines for the
         architecture being developed

## 8.12  Recommended Reading

The following are recommended sources of further information for this
chapter:
- TOGAF 9 Part III: ADM Guidelines and Techniques, Chapter 18
  (Introduction)
- TOGAF 9 Part III: ADM Guidelines and Techniques, Chapter 23
  (Architecture Principles)

- TOGAF 9 Part III: ADM Guidelines and Techniques, Chapter 26 (Business Scenarios)
- TOGAF 9 Part III: ADM Guidelines and Techniques, Chapter 27 (Gap Analysis)
- TOGAF 9 Part III: ADM Guidelines and Techniques, Chapter 29 (Interoperability Requirements)
- TOGAF 9 Part III: ADM Guidelines and Techniques, Chapter 30 (Business Transformation Readiness Assessment)
- TOGAF 9 Part III: ADM Guidelines and Techniques, Chapter 31 (Risk Management)
- TOGAF 9 Part III: ADM Guidelines and Techniques, Chapter 32 (Capability-Based Planning)

Chapter 9

# Architecture Governance

## 9.1 Key Learning Points

This chapter will help you understand Architecture Governance, and how it contributes to the Architecture Development Cycle.

**Key Points Explained**

This chapter will help you to answer the following questions:

- What is Architecture Governance?
- What are the main concepts that make up an Architecture Governance Framework?
- Why is Architecture Governance beneficial?
- What is the need to establish an Architecture Board?
- What are the responsibilities of an Architecture Board?
- What is the role of Architecture Contracts?
- What is Architecture Compliance?
- How can the ADM be used to establish an Architecture Capability?

TOGAF provides significant guidance on establishing effective Architecture Governance and coordinating with other governance processes within the organization. Effective governance ensures that problems are identified early and that subsequent changes to the environment occur in a controlled manner.
[Source: Bill Estrem, "TOGAF to the Rescue" (www.opengroup.org/downloads)]

## 9.2  Introduction to Architecture Governance

*(Syllabus Reference: Unit 8, Learning Outcome 1: You should be able to briefly explain the concept of Architecture Governance.)*

Architecture Governance is the practice by which enterprise architectures and other architectures are managed and controlled at an enterprise-wide level.

Architecture Governance includes the following:
*   Implementing a system of controls over the creation and monitoring of all architectural components and activities, to ensure the effective introduction, implementation, and evolution of architectures within the organization
*   Implementing a system to ensure compliance with internal and external standards and regulatory obligations
*   Establishing processes that support effective management of the above processes within agreed parameters
*   Developing practices that ensure accountability to a clearly identified stakeholder community, both inside and outside the organization

Architecture Governance typically operates within a hierarchy of governance structures which, particularly in the larger enterprise, can include the following as distinct domains with their own disciplines and processes:
*   Corporate Governance
*   Technology Governance
*   IT Governance
*   Architecture Governance

Each of these domains of governance may exist at multiple geographic levels – global, regional, and local – within the overall enterprise. Corporate Governance is a broad topic and outside the scope of the TOGAF framework.

**What is Governance?**

Governance is about ensuring that business is conducted properly. It is less about overt control and strict adherence to rules, and more about effective usage of resources to ensure sustainability of an organization's strategic objectives.

The following characteristics, adapted from Corporate Governance (Naidoo, 2002), are used in TOGAF to highlight both the value and necessity for governance as an approach to be adopted within organizations and their dealings with all involved parties:

**Discipline:** All involved parties will have a commitment to adhere to procedures, processes, and authority structures established by the organization.

**Transparency:** All actions implemented and their decision support will be available for inspection by authorized organization and provider parties.

**Independence:** All processes, decision-making, and mechanisms used will be established so as to minimize or avoid potential conflicts of interest.

**Accountability:** Identifiable groups within the organization – e.g., governance boards who take actions or make decisions – are authorized and accountable for their actions.

**Responsibility:** Each contracted party is required to act responsibly to the organization and its stakeholders.

**Fairness:** All decisions taken, processes used, and their implementation will not be allowed to create unfair advantage to any one particular party.

## 9.3  TOGAF Architecture Governance Framework

*(Syllabus Reference: Unit 8, Learning Outcome 2: You should be able to describe the main concepts that make up an Architecture Governance Framework.)*

Phase G of the TOGAF ADM is dedicated to Implementation Governance, which concerns itself with the realization of the architecture through change projects. Architecture Governance covers the management and control of all aspects of the development and evolution of architectures. It needs to be supported by an Architecture Governance Framework which assists in identifying effective processes so that the business responsibilities associated with Architecture Governance can be elucidated, communicated, and managed effectively. TOGAF provides such a framework, which is described in the following sections.

### 9.3.1  Conceptual Structure

Architecture Governance is an approach, a series of processes, a cultural orientation, and set of owned responsibilities that ensure the integrity and effectiveness of the organization's architectures. The key concepts are shown in Figure 19.

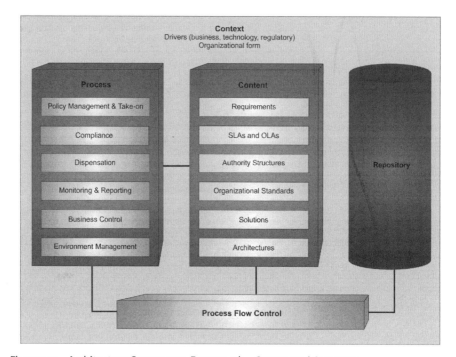

Figure 19:   Architecture Governance Framework – Conceptual Structure

The split of process, content, and context is key to supporting an Architecture Governance initiative. It allows the introduction of new governance material (for example, due to new regulations) without unduly impacting the processes. The content-agnostic approach ensures the framework is flexible.

**Key Architecture Governance Processes**
The following are the key processes:
1.  Policy Management and Take-On
2.  Compliance
3.  Dispensation
4.  Monitoring and Reporting

5.  Business Control

6.  Environment Management

### 9.3.2  Organizational Structure

Governance is the practice of managing and controlling architectures. An effective Architecture Governance structure requires processes, structures, and capabilities (see Figure 20) and will typically include a global governance board, local governance board, design authorities, and working parties.

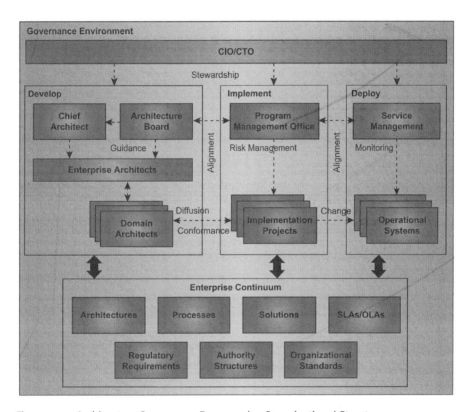

Figure 20:   Architecture Governance Framework – Organizational Structure

## 9.4  The Benefits of Architecture Governance

*(Syllabus Reference: Unit 8, Learning Outcome 3: You should be able to explain why Architecture Governance is beneficial.)*

Architecture Governance is beneficial because it:

- Links IT processes, resources, and information to organizational strategies and objectives

- Integrates and institutionalizes IT best practices
- Aligns with industry frameworks such as COBIT (planning and organizing, acquiring and implementing, delivering and supporting, and monitoring IT performance)
- Enables the organization to take full advantage of its information, infrastructure, and hardware/software assets
- Protects the underlying digital assets of the organization
- Supports regulatory and best practice requirements such as auditability, security, responsibility, and accountability
- Promotes visible risk management

**What are the Key Success Factors when establishing Architecture Governance?**

It is important to consider the following to ensure a successful approach to Architecture Governance, and effective management of the Architecture Contract:

- Establishment and operation of best practices for submission, adoption, re-use, reporting, and retirement of architecture policies, procedures, roles, skills, organizational structures, and support services
- Establishment of correct organizational responsibilities and structures to support Architecture Governance processes and reporting requirements
- Integration of tools and processes to facilitate take-up of processes (both procedural and cultural)
- Management of criteria for control of Architecture Governance processes, dispensations, compliance assessments, Service Level Agreements (SLAs), and Operational Level Agreements (OLAs)
- Meeting internal and external requirements for effectiveness, efficiency, confidentiality, integrity, availability, compliance, and reliability of Architecture Governance-related information, services, and processes

## 9.5  Architecture Board

*(Syllabus Reference: Unit 8, Learning Outcome 4: You should be able to briefly explain the need for establishment of an Architecture Board.)*

An enterprise architecture imposed without appropriate political backing is bound to fail. An important element in any Architecture Governance strategy is establishment of a cross-organizational Architecture Board to oversee the implementation of the governance strategy. This body should be representative of all the key stakeholders in the architecture, and will typically comprise a group of executives responsible for the review and maintenance of the overall architecture.

*(Syllabus Reference: Unit 8, Learning Outcome 5: You should be able to list the responsibilities of an Architecture Board.)*

The Architecture Board is typically made responsible, and accountable, for achieving some or all of the following goals:
- Providing the basis for all decision-making with regard to changes to the architectures
- Consistency between sub-architectures
- Establishing targets for re-use of components
- Flexibility of enterprise architecture; to meet business needs and utilize new technologies
- Enforcement of Architecture Compliance
- Improving the maturity level of architecture discipline within the organization
- Ensuring that the discipline of architecture-based development is adopted
- Supporting a visible escalation capability for out-of-bounds decisions

The Architecture Board is also responsible for operational items such as the monitoring and control of Architecture Contracts, and for governance items such as producing usable governance materials.

## 9.6  Architecture Contracts
*(Syllabus Reference: Unit 8, Learning Outcome 6: You should be able to briefly explain the role of Architecture Contracts.)*

Architecture Contracts are joint agreements between development partners and sponsors on the deliverables, quality, and fitness-for-purpose of an architecture. Successful implementation of these agreements will be delivered through effective Architecture Governance. Taking a governed approach to contract management ensures a system that continuously monitors integrity, changes, decision-making, and audit, as well as adherence to the principles, standards, and requirements of the enterprise. The architecture team may also be included in product procurement, to help minimize the opportunity for misinterpretation of the enterprise architecture.

## 9.7 Architecture Compliance

### 9.7.1 The Meaning of Architecture Compliance
*(Syllabus Reference: Unit 8, Learning Outcome 7: You should be able to briefly explain the meaning of Architecture Compliance.)*

TOGAF defines the meaning of key terms such as "conformant", "compliant", etc. as shown in Figure 21.

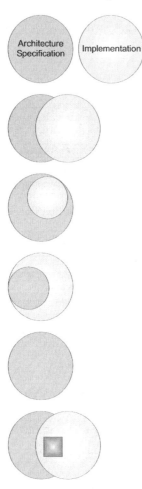

**Irrelevant:**
The implementation has no features in common with the architecture specification (so the question of conformance does not arise).

**Consistent:**
The implementation has some features in common with the architecture specification, and those common features are implemented in accordance with the specification. However, some features in the architecture specification are not implemented, and the implementation has other features that are not covered by the specification.

**Compliant:**
Some features in the architecture specification are not implemented, but all features implemented are covered by the specification, and in accordance with it.

**Conformant:**
All the features in the architecture specification are implemented in accordance with the specification, but some more features are implemented that are not in accordance with it.

**Fully Conformant:**
There is full correspondence between architecture specification and implementation. All specified features are implemented in accordance with the specification, and there are no features implemented that are not covered by the specification.

**Non-conformant:**
Any of the above in which some features in the architecture specification are implemented not in accordance with the specification.

Figure 21: Levels of Architecture Conformance

### 9.7.2 The Need for Architecture Compliance

*(Syllabus Reference: Unit 8, Learning Outcome 8: You should be able to briefly explain the need for Architecture Compliance.)*

Ensuring the compliance of individual projects within the enterprise architecture is an essential aspect of Architecture Governance. An Architecture Compliance strategy should be adopted. TOGAF recommends two complementary processes:

- The Architecture function will be required to prepare a series of Project Architectures; i.e., project-specific views of the enterprise architecture that illustrate how the enterprise architecture impacts on the major projects within the organization. (See ADM Phases A to F.)
- The IT Governance function will define a formal Architecture Compliance Review process (see below) for reviewing the compliance of projects to the enterprise architecture.

Apart from defining formal processes, the Architecture Governance function may also stipulate that the architecture function should extend beyond the role of architecture definition and standards selection, and participate also in the technology selection process, and even in the commercial relationships involved in external service provision and product purchases. This may help to minimize the opportunity for misinterpretation of the enterprise architecture, and maximize the value of centralized commercial negotiation.

### 9.7.3 The Purpose of Architecture Compliance Reviews

*(Syllabus Reference: Unit 8, Learning Outcome 9: You should be able to briefly explain the purpose of Architecture Compliance Reviews.)*

The purpose of an Architecture Compliance Review includes the following:

- To catch errors in the project architecture early, and thereby reduce the cost and risk of changes required later in the lifecycle; this in turn means that the overall project time is shortened, and that the business gets the bottom-line benefit of the architecture development faster
- To ensure the application of best practices to architecture work
- To provide an overview of the compliance of an architecture to mandated enterprise standards
- To identify where the standards themselves may require modification
- To identify services that are currently application-specific but might be provided as part of the enterprise infrastructure

- To document strategies for collaboration, resource sharing, and other synergies across multiple architecture teams
- To take advantage of advances in technology
- To communicate to management the status of technical readiness of the project
- To identify key criteria for procurement activities (e.g., for inclusion in Commercial Off-The-Shelf (COTS) product RFI/RFP documents)
- To identify and communicate significant architectural gaps to product and service providers

The Architecture Compliance Review can also be a good way of deciding between architectural alternatives, since the business decision-makers typically involved in the review can guide decisions in terms of what is best for the business, as opposed to what is technically more pleasing or elegant.

### 9.7.4  The Architecture Compliance Review Process

*(Syllabus Reference: Unit 8, Learning Outcome 10: You should be able to briefly describe the Architecture Compliance Review process.)*

An Architecture Compliance Review is a scrutiny of the compliance of a specific project against established architectural criteria, spirit, and business objectives. TOGAF describes a process, including the roles and actions to undertake a review and deliver an assessment report, as summarized in Figure 22.

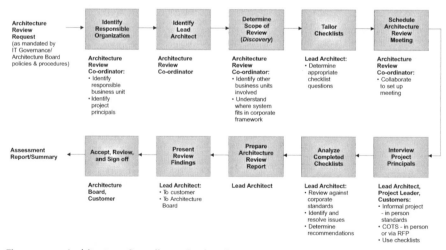

Figure 22:   Architecture Compliance Review Process

This consists of 12 steps as follows:

| Step | Action | Notes | Who |
| --- | --- | --- | --- |
| 1 | Request Architecture Review | Mandated by governance policies | Anyone with an interest in or responsibility for the business area |
| 2 | Identify responsible part of organization and project principals | | Architecture Review Co-ordinator |
| 3 | Identify Lead Enterprise Architect and other architects | | Architecture Review Co-ordinator |
| 4 | Determine scope of review | Identify which other business units/departments are involved Understand where the system fits into the corporate architecture framework | Architecture Review Co-ordinator |
| 5 | Tailor checklists | To address the business requirements | Lead Enterprise Architect |
| 6 | Schedule Architecture Review meeting | | Architecture Review Co-ordinator with collaboration of Lead Enterprise Architect |
| 7 | Interview project principals | To get background and technical information For internal project: in person For COTS: in person or via RFP Use checklists | Lead Enterprise Architect, and/ or Architect, Project Leader, and Customers |
| 8 | Analyze completed checklists | Review against corporate standards Identify and resolve issues Determine recommendations | Lead Enterprise Architect |
| 9 | Prepare Architecture Compliance Review report | May involve supporting staff | Lead Enterprise Architect |
| 10 | Present review findings | To Customer To Architecture Board | Lead Enterprise Architect |

| Step | Action | Notes | Who |
|------|--------|-------|-----|
| 11 | Accept review and sign-off | | Architecture Board and Customer |
| 12 | Send assessment report/ summary to Architecture Review Co-ordinator | | Lead Enterprise Architect |

## 9.8 Using the ADM to Establish an Architecture Capability

*(Syllabus Reference: Unit 8, Learning Outcome 11: You should be able to briefly explain how the ADM can be used to establish an Architecture Capability.)*

Establishing a sustainable Architecture Capability within an organization can be achieved by adhering to the same approach that is used to establish any other capability – such as a business process management capability – within an organization. The ADM is an ideal method to be used to architect and govern the implementation of such a capability. Applying the ADM with the specific Architecture Vision to establish an architecture practice within the organization would achieve this objective.

TOGAF states that this should not be seen as a phase of an architecture project, or a one-off project, but rather as an ongoing practice that provides the context, environment, and resources to govern and enable architecture delivery to the organization. As an architecture project is executed within this environment it might request a change to the architecture practice that would trigger another cycle of the ADM to extend the architecture practice.

Implementing any capability within an organization would require the design of the four domain architectures: Business, Data, Application, and Technology. Establishing the architecture practice within an organization would therefore require the design of:

- The Business Architecture of the architecture practice that will highlight the Architecture Governance, architecture processes, architecture organizational structure, architecture information requirements, architecture products, etc.
- The Data Architecture that would define the structure of the organization's Enterprise Continuum and Architecture Repository

- The Application Architecture specifying the functionality and/or applications services required to enable the architecture practice
- The Technology Architecture that depicts the architecture practice's infrastructure requirements and deployment in support of the architecture applications and Enterprise Continuum

## 9.9 Summary

Architecture Governance is the practice and orientation by which enterprise architectures and other architectures are managed and controlled at an enterprise-wide level. It includes the following:

- Implementing a system of controls over the creation and monitoring of all architecture components and activities, to ensure the effective introduction, implementation, and evolution of architectures within the organization
- Implementing a system to ensure compliance with internal and external standards and regulatory obligations
- Establishing processes that support effective management of the above processes within agreed parameters
- Developing practices that ensure accountability to a clearly identified stakeholder community, both inside and outside the organization

An important element in any Architecture Governance strategy is establishment of a cross-organizational Architecture Board to oversee the implementation of the governance strategy. This body should be representative of all the key stakeholders in the architecture, and will typically comprise a group of executives responsible for the review and maintenance of the overall architecture.

Architecture Contracts are joint agreements between development partners and sponsors on the deliverables, quality, and fitness-for-purpose of an architecture. Successful implementation of these agreements will be delivered through effective Architecture Governance.

Ensuring the compliance of individual projects within the enterprise architecture is an essential aspect of Architecture Governance. An Architecture Compliance strategy should be adopted.

## 9.10  Test Yourself Questions

Q1:  Which of the following statements about Architecture Governance is not correct?

    A.  It is the practice and orientation by which enterprise architectures and other architectures are managed and controlled.

    B.  The Chief Architect manages the Architecture Governance activity.

    C.  An Architecture Governance Framework supports it.

    D.  It is a set of owned responsibilities that ensure the integrity and effectiveness of the organization's architecture.

Q2:  The following are included in Architecture Governance, except:

    A.  Implementing a system of controls over expenditure within the enterprise

    B.  Implementing a system of controls over the creation and monitoring of all architecture components and activities

    C.  Implementing a system to ensure compliance with internal and external standards and regulatory obligations

    D.  Establishing processes that support effective management of the Architecture Governance process

    E.  Developing practices that ensure accountability to stakeholders

Q3:  Which of the following maps to the characteristic "transparency"?

    A.  All decisions taken, processes used, and their implementation will not be allowed to create unfair advantage to any one particular party.

    B.  Each contractual party is required to act responsibly to the organization and its shareholders.

    C.  All actions implemented and their decision support will be available for inspection by authorized organization and provider parties.

    D.  All involved parties will have a commitment to adhere to procedures, processes, and authority structures established by the organization.

    E.  All processes, decision-making, and mechanisms used will be established so as to minimize or avoid potential conflicts of interest.

Q4: Conceptually, the structure of an Architecture Governance Framework consists of process, content, and context (stored in the repository). The following are included in content, except:

A. Compliance

B. SLAs and OLAs

C. Organizational standards

D. Regulatory requirements

E. Architectures

Q5: The following are key Architecture Governance processes, except:

A. Compliance

B. Dispensation

C. Monitoring and reporting

D. Budgetary control

E. Business control

Q6: Why is Architecture Governance beneficial?

A. It links IT processes, resources, and information to organizational strategies and objectives.

B. It integrates and institutionalizes IT best practices.

C. It enables the organization to take full advantage of its information, infrastructure, and hardware/software assets.

D. It protects the underlying digital assets of the organization.

E. All of these.

Q7: Which one of the following is not the responsibility of an Architecture Board?

A. Resourcing of architecture projects

B. Decision-making with regards to changes to the architectures

C. Enforcement of Architecture Compliance

D. Monitoring of Architecture Contracts

Q8: Which one of the following best describes an Architecture Contract?

A. An agreement between the development partners and stakeholders on the acceptable risks and mitigating actions for an architecture

B. An agreement between development partners and sponsors on the deliverables, quality, and fitness-for-purpose of an architecture

C.  An agreement between the lead architect and the development partners on the enforcement of Architecture Compliance for an architecture

D.  An agreement between development partners and sponsors on how best to monitor implementation of the architecture

Q9:  TOGAF defines a set of terms to describe Architecture Compliance. Which one of the following applies to the case where an implementation has no features in common with the architecture specification?

A.  Compliant

B.  Conformant

C.  Irrelevant

D.  Non-conformant

Q10:  In an Architecture Compliance Review, who is responsible for accepting and signing off on the review?

A.  Architecture Board

B.  Architecture Review Co-ordinator

C.  Lead Enterprise Architect

D.  Project Leader

Q11:  When using the ADM to establish an Architecture Capability, which phase would define the infrastructure requirements to support the practice?

A.  Application Architecture

B.  Business Architecture

C.  Data Architecture

D.  Technology Architecture

## 9.11 Recommended Reading

The following are recommended sources of further information for this chapter:

- TOGAF 9 Part VII: Architecture Capability Framework, Chapter 46 (Establishing an Architecture Capability)
- TOGAF 9 Part VII: Architecture Capability Framework, Chapter 47 (Architecture Board)
- TOGAF 9 Part VII: Architecture Capability Framework, Chapter 48 (Architecture Compliance)
- TOGAF 9 Part VII: Architecture Capability Framework, Chapter 49 (Architecture Contracts)
- TOGAF 9 Part VII: Architecture Capability Framework, Chapter 50 (Architecture Governance)

Chapter 10

# Views, Viewpoints, and Stakeholders

## 10.1 Key Learning Points

This chapter will help you understand the concepts of views and viewpoints, and their role in communicating with stakeholders.

**Key Points Explained**

This chapter will help you to answer the following questions:

- What are the key concepts for views and viewpoints in TOGAF?
- How can a simple example of a viewpoint and view be described?
- What are the relationships between stakeholders, concerns, views, and viewpoints?
- How are views created?

## 10.2 Concepts and Definitions

*(Syllabus Reference: Unit 9, Learning Outcome 1: You should be able to define and explain the following concepts: stakeholders, concerns, views and viewpoints.)*

In this section we introduce the following concepts and definitions:

- System
- Stakeholders
- Concerns
- Views
- Viewpoints

These have been adapted from more formal definitions in ISO/IEC 42010:2007. Many people use these terms in different ways. Here we need to understand them within the context of TOGAF 9.

### 10.2.1 System

A *system* is a collection of components organized to accomplish a specific function or set of functions.

"The term *system* encompasses individual applications, systems in the traditional sense, subsystems, systems of systems, product lines, product families, whole enterprises, and other aggregations of interest."

[Source: ISO/IEC 42010:2007, previously known as IEEE Std 1471-2000]

### 10.2.2  Stakeholders

*Stakeholders* are people who have key roles in, or *concerns* about, the system; for example, users, developers, etc. Stakeholders can be individuals, teams, organizations, etc.

A system has one or more stakeholders. Each stakeholder typically has interests in, or concerns relative to, that system. Figure 2326 shows a typical set of stakeholders for an enterprise architecture, with defined categories of stakeholder type.

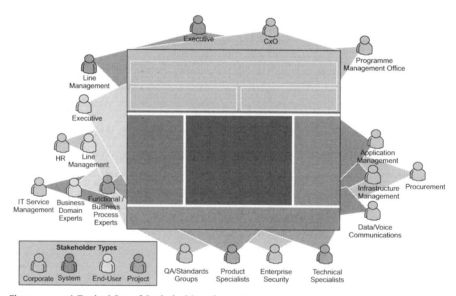

Figure 23:    A Typical Set of Stakeholders for an Enterprise Architecture

### 10.2.3  Concerns

*Concerns* are key interests that are crucially important to stakeholders, and determine the acceptability of the system.

They may include performance, reliability, security, distribution, evolvability, etc. A Security Architect could have the following concerns: authentication, authorization, audit, assurance, availability, asset protection, administration, risk management.

> The terms "concern" and "requirement" are not synonymous. A concern is an area of interest.
>
> Concerns are the root of the process of decomposition into requirements.
>
> Concerns are represented in the architecture by these requirements. Requirements should be SMART (i.e., should include specific metrics).
>
> [Source: TOGAF 9 Part VI: Architecture Content Framework, Chapter 35 (Architectural Artifacts)]

### 10.2.4  View

A *view* is a representation of a system from the perspective of a related set of concerns. A view is what you see (or what a stakeholder sees).

An architect creates architecture models. A view consists of parts of these, chosen to show stakeholders that their concerns are being met. For example, just as a building architect will create wiring diagrams, floor plans, and elevations to describe different facets of a building to its different stakeholders (electricians, owners, planning officials), so an Enterprise Architect must create different views of the business, information system, and technical architecture for the stakeholders who have concerns related to these aspects. These might include business process, physical layout, and security views of an IT system.

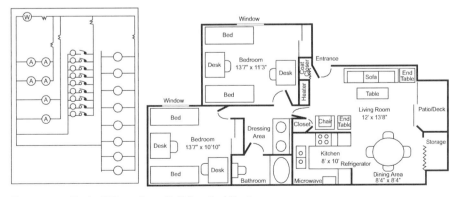

Figure 24:   Typical Views from Building Architecture

### 10.2.5  Viewpoint

A *viewpoint* defines the perspective from which a view is taken.

It defines how to construct and use a view, the information needed, the modeling techniques for expressing and analyzing it, and a rationale for these choices (e.g., by describing the purpose and intended audience of the view).

The relationship between viewpoint and view is analogous to that of a template and an instance of the completed template. In constructing an enterprise architecture, an architect first selects the viewpoints (templates), then constructs a set of corresponding views (instances).

## 10.3  Architecture Views and Viewpoints

*(Syllabus Reference: Unit 9, Learning Outcome 2: You should be able to describe a simple example of a viewpoint and view.)*

The architect uses views and viewpoints in the ADM cycle during Phases A through D for developing architectures for each domain (Business, Data, Application, and Technology).

> **Views and Viewpoints**
>
> A "view" is what you see. A "viewpoint" is where you are looking from; the vantage point or perspective that determines what you see (a viewpoint can also be thought of as a schema).
>
> Viewpoints are generic, and can be stored in libraries for re-use.
>
> A view is always specific to the architecture for which it is created.
>
> Every view has an associated viewpoint that describes it, at least implicitly.

To illustrate the concepts of views and viewpoints, consider Example 3. This is a very simple airport system with two different stakeholders: the pilot and the air traffic controller.

Example 3:  Views and Viewpoints for a Simple Airport System

> **Views and Viewpoints for a Simple Airport System**
>
> The pilot has one view of the system, and the air traffic controller has another. Neither view represents the whole system, because the perspective of each stakeholder constrains (and reduces) how each sees the overall system.
>
> The view of the pilot comprises some elements not viewed by the controller, such as passengers and fuel, while the view of the controller comprises some elements not viewed by the pilot, such as other planes. There are also elements shared between the views, such as the communication model between the pilot and the controller, and the vital information about the plane itself.
>
> A viewpoint is a model (or description) of the information contained in a view. In this example, one viewpoint is the description of how the pilot sees the system, and the other viewpoint is how the controller sees the system. Pilots describe the system from their perspective, using a model of their position and vector toward or away from the runway. All pilots use this model, and the model has a specific language that is used to capture information and populate the model. Controllers describe the system differently, using a model of the airspace and the locations and vectors of aircraft within the airspace. Again, all controllers use a common language derived from the common model in order to capture and communicate information pertinent to their viewpoint.
>
> Fortunately, when controllers talk with pilots, they use a common communication language. (In other words, the models representing their individual viewpoints partially intersect.) Part of this common language is about location and vectors of aircraft, and is essential to safety. So in essence each viewpoint is an abstract model of how all the stakeholders of a particular type – all pilots, or all controllers – view the airport system. The interface to the human user of a tool is typically close to the model and language associated with the viewpoint. The unique tools of the pilot are fuel, altitude, speed, and location indicators. The main tool of the controller is radar. The common tool is a radio.

To summarize from Example 3, we can see that a view can subset the system through the perspective of the stakeholder, such as the pilot *versus* the controller. This subset can be described by an abstract model called a viewpoint, such as an air flight *versus* an air space model. This description of the view is documented in a partially specialized language, such as "pilot-speak" *versus* "controller-speak". Tools are used to assist the stakeholders, and they interface with each other in terms of the language derived from the viewpoint. When stakeholders use common tools, such as the radio contact between pilot and controller, a common language is essential.

For many architectures, a useful viewpoint is that of business domains, which can be illustrated by an example from The Open Group.

The viewpoint can be specified as follows:

| Viewpoint Element | Description |
|---|---|
| Stakeholders | Management Board, Chief Executive Officer |
| Concerns | Show the top-level relationships between geographical sites and business functions. |
| Modeling technique | Nested boxes diagram.<br>Outer boxes = locations; inner boxes = business functions.<br>Semantics of nesting = functions performed in the locations. |

The corresponding view of The Open Group (in 2008) is shown in Figure 25.

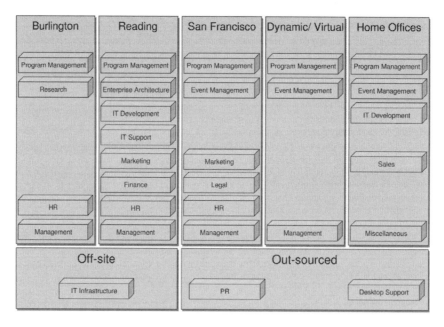

Figure 25:   Example View – The Open Group Business Domains

## 10.4 The Relationship between Stakeholders, Concerns, Views, and Viewpoints

*(Syllabus Reference: Unit 9, Learning Outcome 3: You should be able to discuss the relationship between stakeholders, concerns, views, and viewpoints.)*

The relationship between stakeholders, concerns, views, and viewpoints are summarized in Figure 26.[11]

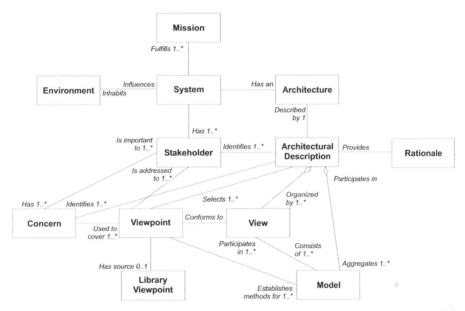

Figure 26:    Relationship between Basic Architectural Concepts

## 10.5 The View Creation Process

*(Syllabus Reference: Unit 9, Learning Outcome 4: You should be able to describe the view creation process.)*

---

11    Reprinted with permission from IEEE Std 1471-2000, Systems and Software Engineering – Recommended Practice for Architectural Description of Software-Intensive Systems, Copyright © 2000, by the IEEE.

> Architecture views are representations of the overall architecture in terms
> meaningful to stakeholders. They enable the architecture to be communicated
> to and understood by the stakeholders, so they can verify that the system will
> address their concerns.
> [Source: TOGAF 9 Part IV: Architecture Content Framework, Chapter 35
> (Architectural Artifacts)]

The architect chooses and develops a set of views in the ADM cycle during
Phases A through D that enable the architecture to be communicated to, and
understood by, all the stakeholders, and enable them to verify that the system
will address their concerns.

The choice of which particular architecture views to develop is one of the key
decisions that the architect has to make.
The architect has a responsibility for ensuring:
- The completeness of the architecture:
  — Does it address all the concerns of its stakeholders?
- The integrity of the architecture:
  — Can the views be connected to each other?
  — Can the conflicting concerns be reconciled?
  — What trade-offs have been made (e.g., between security and
    performance)?

**Recommended Steps**
The following are the recommended steps to create the required views for a
particular architecture:
1. Refer to any existing libraries of viewpoints (note that TOGAF 9 includes
   a set of architecture viewpoints).
2. Select key stakeholders.
3. Analyze their concerns and document them.
4. Select appropriate viewpoints (based on the stakeholders and their
   concerns).
5. Generate views of the system using the selected viewpoints as templates.

## 10.6 Summary

TOGAF embraces the concepts and definitions of ISO/IEC 42010:2007, specifically those that guide the development of a view, and make the view actionable, such as:

- Selecting key stakeholders
- Analyzing their concerns and documenting them
- Understanding how to model and deal with those concerns

The language used to depict the view is the viewpoint. The viewpoints provided should be customized to create a set of architecture views that ensure all stakeholder concerns are met.

## 10.7 Test Yourself Questions

Q1: Which of the following terms does TOGAF use to describe people who have key roles in, or concerns about, a system?

    A. Architect

    B. Consumer

    C. Customer

    D. Sponsor

    E. Stakeholder

Q2: Which of the following statements is not correct?

    A. A view can be thought of as a template for a viewpoint.

    B. A viewpoint defines the perspective from which a view is taken.

    C. A viewpoint defines how to construct and use a view.

    D. A view is what a stakeholder sees.

    E. A view might describe business process for an IT system.

Q3: Which of the following statements is not correct?

    A. A concern might include performance and reliability.

    B. A concern is an area of interest.

    C. Concerns are key interests of the stakeholders.

    D. Concern and requirement are synonymous.

Q4:   In Example 3, Views and Viewpoints for a Simple Airport System,
      which of the following is the common tool used by pilots and
      controllers?
      A.   Altitude
      B.   Fuel
      C.   Location
      D.   Radar
      E.   Radio

Q5:   Which of the following statements describing relationships between
      stakeholders, concerns, views, and viewpoints is correct?
      A.   A concern is important to only one stakeholder.
      B.   A stakeholder identifies one or more concerns.
      C.   A viewpoint covers one concern.
      D.   A viewpoint consists of one or more views.

## 10.8  Recommended Reading

The following are recommended sources of further information for this
chapter:

- TOGAF 9 Part IV: Architecture Content Framework, Chapter 35
  (Architectural Artifacts)

# Chapter 11

# Building Blocks

## 11.1 Key Learning Points

This chapter will help you understand the concept of building blocks within TOGAF.

**Key Points Explained**

This chapter will help you to answer the following questions:
- What is a building block?
- What is the difference between an Architecture Building Block and a Solution Building Block?
- How are building blocks used within the ADM cycle?
- What are the characteristics of an architecture pattern?

## 11.2 What is a Building Block?

*(Syllabus Reference: Unit 10, Learning Outcome 1: You should be able to define what a building block is, and explain what makes a good building block.)*

A building block is a package of functionality defined to meet business needs across an organization. A building block has published interfaces to access functionality. A building block may interoperate with other, possibly inter-dependent building blocks.

A good building block has the following characteristics:
- It considers implementation and usage, and evolves to exploit technology and standards.
- It may be assembled from other building blocks.
- It may be a subassembly of other building blocks.
- Ideally, a building block is re-usable and replaceable, and well specified with stable interfaces.
- Its specification should be loosely coupled to its implementation, so that it can be realized in several ways without impacting the building block specification.

The way in which functionality, products, and custom developments are assembled into building blocks varies widely between individual architectures. Every organization must decide for itself what arrangement of building blocks works best for it. A good choice of building blocks can lead to improvements in legacy system integration, interoperability, and flexibility in the creation of new systems and applications.

An architecture is a composition of:
- A set of building blocks depicted in an architectural model
- A specification of how those building blocks are connected to meet the overall requirements of an information system

The various building blocks in an architecture specify the services required in an enterprise-specific system.

The following general principles should apply:
- An architecture need only contain building blocks to implement those services it requires.
- Building blocks may implement one, more than one, or only part of a service identified in the architecture.
- Building blocks should conform to standards.

## 11.3  Architecture Building Blocks and Solution Building Blocks

*(Syllabus Reference: Unit 10, Learning Outcome 2: You should be able to explain the distinction between Architecture Building Blocks and Solution Building Blocks.)*

Systems are built from collections of buildings blocks. They can be defined at many levels of detail:
- Groupings at a functional level, such as a customer database, are known as Architecture Building Blocks.
- Real products or specific custom developments are known as Solutions Building Blocks.

### 11.3.1  Architecture Building Blocks

Architecture Building Blocks (ABBs) are architecture documentation and models from the enterprise's Architecture Repository classified according to the Architecture Continuum. They are defined or selected during application of the ADM – mainly in Phases A, B, C, and D.

The characteristics of ABBs are as follows:
- They define what functionality will be implemented.
- They capture architecture requirements; e.g., Business, Data, Application, and Technology requirements.
- They direct and guide the development of Solution Building Blocks.

ABB specifications should contain as a minimum:
- Fundamental functionality and attributes: semantic, unambiguous, including security capability and manageability
- Interfaces: chosen set, supplied
- Interoperability and relationship to other building blocks
- Dependent building blocks with required functionality and named user interfaces
- Map to business/organizational entities and policies

Each ABB should include a statement of any architecture documentation and models from the enterprise's Architecture Repository that can be re-used in the architecture development. The specification of building blocks using the ADM is an evolutionary and iterative process.

### 11.3.2  Solution Building Blocks

Solution Building Blocks (SBBs) relate to the Solutions Continuum. They are implementations of the architectures identified in the enterprise's Architecture Continuum and may be either procured or developed. SBBs appear in Phase E of the ADM where product-specific building blocks are considered for the first time. SBBs define what products and components will implement the functionality, thereby defining the implementation.

The characteristics of SBBs are as follows:
- They define what products and components will implement the functionality.
- They define the implementation.

- They fulfill business requirements.
- They are product or vendor-aware.

SBB specifications should contain as a minimum:
- Specific functionality and attributes
- Interfaces: the implemented set
- Required SBBs used with required functionality and names of interfaces used
- Mapping from the SBBs to the IT topology and operational policies
- Specifications of attributes shared such as security, manageability, scalability
- Performance, configurability
- Design drivers and constraints including physical architecture
- Relationships between the SBBs and ABBs

## 11.4  Building Blocks and the ADM

*(Syllabus Reference: Unit 10, Learning Outcome 3: You should be able to briefly explain the use of building blocks in the ADM cycle.)*

Systems are built up from collections of building blocks, so most building blocks have to interoperate with other building blocks. Wherever that is true, it is important that the interfaces to a building block are published and reasonably stable.

Building blocks can be defined at various levels of detail, depending on what stage of architecture development has been reached.

For instance, at an early stage, a building block can simply consist of a grouping of functionality, such as a customer database and some retrieval tools. Building blocks at this functional level of definition are described in TOGAF as Architecture Building Blocks (ABBs). Later on, real products or custom developments replace these simple definitions of functionality, and the building blocks are then described as Solution Building Blocks (SBBs).

The key phases and steps of the ADM at which building blocks are evolved and specified are summarized as follows, and illustrated in Figure 27.

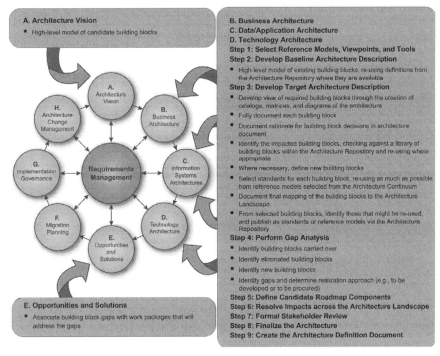

Figure 27:    Architecture Building Blocks and their Use in the ADM Cycle

In Phase A, the earliest building block definitions start as relatively abstract entities within the Architecture Vision.

In Phases B, C, and D building blocks within the Business, Data, Application, and Technology Architectures are evolved to a common pattern of steps. Finally, in Phase E the building blocks become more implementation-specific as SBBs are identified to address gaps.

## 11.5  Architecture Patterns

*(Syllabus Reference: Unit 10, Learning Outcome 4: You should be able to describe the characteristics of an architecture pattern.)*

**Pattern**

A pattern is "an idea that has been useful in one practical context and will probably be useful in others".

[Source: Analysis Patterns – Re-usable Object Models]

In TOGAF, patterns are considered to be a way of putting building blocks into context; for example, to describe a re-usable solution to a problem. Building blocks are what you use; patterns can tell you how you use them, when, why, and what trade-offs you have to make in doing that.

Patterns offer the promise of helping the architect to identify combinations of Architecture and/or Solution Building Blocks (ABBs/SBBs) that have been proven to deliver effective solutions in the past, and may provide the basis for effective solutions in the future.

## 11.6 Summary

A building block has the following characteristics:
- It is a package of functionality defined to meet the business needs across an organization
- It has published interfaces to access functionality
- It may interoperate with other, inter-dependent building blocks

A good building block:
- Considers implementation and usage and evolves to exploit technology
- May be assembled from other building blocks
- Is re-usable

## 11.7 Test Yourself Questions

Q1:   Which of the following statements does not apply to a building block?
    A.   It is a package of functionality that meets business needs.
    B.   It has published interfaces to access functionality.
    C.   It may interoperate with other building blocks.
    D.   It has a specification that is tightly coupled to its implementation.

Q2:   Which of the following applies to an Architecture Building Block?
    A.   It defines the functionality to be implemented.
    B.   It defines the implementation.
    C.   It defines what products and components will implement the functionality.
    D.   It is product or vendor-aware.

Q3:   Which of the following ADM phases is where SBBs first appear in the
      ADM cycle?
      A.   Phase A
      B.   Phase B
      C.   Phase D
      D.   Phase E
      E.   Phase G

## 11.8  Recommended Reading

The following are recommended sources of further information for this
chapter:

- TOGAF 9 Part IV: Architecture Content Framework, Chapter 37
  (Building Blocks)

# Chapter 12

# ADM Deliverables

## 12.1 Key Learning Points

This chapter will help you understand the key terminology of TOGAF.

**Key Points Explained**

This chapter will help you to answer the following questions:
- What is the role of architecture deliverables across the ADM cycle?
- What is the purpose of key deliverables?

## 12.2 The Role of Architecture Deliverables

*(Syllabus Reference: Unit 11, Learning Outcome 1: You should be able to briefly explain the role of architecture deliverables across the ADM cycle.)*

TOGAF defines a set of suggested deliverables that will be consumed and produced across the TOGAF ADM cycle The deliverable set provided is intended to provide a typical baseline of architecture deliverables in order to better define the activities required in the ADM and act as a starting point for tailoring within a specific organization.

TOGAF identifies deliverables that are produced as outputs from executing the ADM cycle and potentially consumed as inputs at other points in the ADM. Other deliverables may be produced elsewhere and consumed by the ADM.

> As deliverables are typically the contractual or formal work products of an architecture project, it is likely that these deliverables will be constrained or altered by any overarching project or process management for the enterprise (such as CMMI, PRINCE2, PMBOK, or MSP).
> [Source: TOGAF 9 Part IV: Architecture Content Framework]

## 12.3 The Purpose of Key Deliverables

*(Syllabus Reference: Unit 11, Learning Outcome 2: For each of the deliverables in this section, you should be able to briefly explain the purpose of the deliverable.)*

This section describes the purpose of deliverables consumed and produced across the TOGAF ADM cycle.

### 12.3.1 Architecture Building Blocks (ABBs)

ABBs are architecture documentation and models from the enterprise's Architecture Repository.
See Chapter 11.

### 12.3.2 Architecture Contract

Architecture Contracts are the joint agreements between development partners and sponsors on the deliverables, quality, and fitness-for-purpose of an architecture. They are produced in Phase G: Architecture Governance. Successful implementation of these agreements will be delivered through effective Architecture Governance.

By implementing a governed approach to the management of contracts, the following will be ensured:

- A system of continuous monitoring to check integrity, changes, decision-making, and audit of all architecture-related activities within the organization
- Adherence to the principles, standards, and requirements of the existing or developing architectures
- Identification of risks in all aspects of the development and implementation of the architecture(s) covering the internal development against accepted standards, policies, technologies, and products as well as the operational aspects of the architectures such that the organization can continue its business within a resilient environment
- A set of processes and practices that ensure accountability, responsibility, and discipline with regard to the development and usage of all architectural artifacts
- A formal understanding of the governance organization responsible for the contract, their level of authority, and scope of the architecture under the governance of this body

### 12.3.3  Architecture Definition Document

The Architecture Definition Document is the deliverable container for the core architectural artifacts created during a project and for important related information. The Architecture Definition Document spans all architecture domains (Business, Data, Application, and Technology) and also examines all relevant states of the architecture (baseline, transition, and target).

It is first created in Phase A, where it is populated with artifacts created to support the Architecture Vision. It is updated in Phase B, with Business Architecture-related material, and subsequently updated with Information Systems Architecture material in Phase C, and then with Technology Architecture material in Phase D. Where the scope of change to implement the Target Architecture requires an incremental approach, the Architecture Definition Document will be updated to include one or more Transition Architectures in Phase E.

A Transition Architecture shows the enterprise at an architecturally significant state between the Baseline and Target Architectures. Transition Architectures are used to describe transitional Target Architectures necessary for effective realization of the Target Architecture.

**Architecture Definition Document versus Architecture Requirements Specification**

The Architecture Definition Document is a companion to the Architecture Requirements Specification, with a complementary objective:

The Architecture Definition Document provides a qualitative view of the solution and aims to communicate the intent of the architects.

The Architecture Requirements Specification provides a quantitative view of the solution, stating measurable criteria that must be met during the implementation of the architecture.

### 12.3.4  Architecture Principles

This set of documentation is an initial output of the Preliminary Phase. Principles are general rules and guidelines, intended to be enduring and seldom amended, that inform and support the way in which an organization sets about fulfilling its mission.

In their turn, principles may be just one element in a structured set of ideas that collectively define and guide the organization, from values through actions to results.

See Section 8.3.

### 12.3.5  Architecture Repository

The Architecture Repository acts as a holding area for all architecture-related projects within the enterprise. The repository allows projects to manage their deliverables, locate re-usable assets, and publish outputs to stakeholders and other interested parties.

See Sections 3.5 and 6.8.

### 12.3.6  Architecture Requirements Specification

The Architecture Requirements Specification provides a set of quantitative statements that outline what an implementation project must do in order to comply with the architecture. An Architecture Requirements Specification will typically form a major component of an implementation contract or a contract for more detailed Architecture Definition.

### 12.3.7  Architecture Roadmap

The Architecture Roadmap lists individual work packages that will realize the Target Architecture and lays them out on a timeline to show progression from the Baseline Architecture to the Target Architecture. The Architecture Roadmap highlights individual work packages' business value at each stage. Transition Architectures necessary to effectively realize the Target Architecture are identified as intermediate steps. The Architecture Roadmap is incrementally developed throughout Phases E and F, and informed by the roadmap components developed in Phases B, C, and D.

### 12.3.8  Architecture Vision

The Architecture Vision is created in Phase A and provides a high-level summary of the changes to the enterprise that will follow from successful deployment of the Target Architecture. The purpose of the vision is to agree at the outset what the desired outcome should be for the architecture, so that architects can then focus on the detail necessary to validate feasibility. Providing an Architecture Vision also supports stakeholder communication by providing a summary version of the full Architecture Definition.

Business scenarios (see Section 8.4) are a recommended technique that can be used as part of developing an Architecture Vision document.

### 12.3.9 Business Principles, Business Goals, and Business Drivers

Business principles, business goals, and business drivers provide context for architecture work, by describing the needs and ways of working employed by the enterprise. These will have usually been defined elsewhere in the enterprise prior to the architecture activity. Many factors that lie outside the consideration of architecture discipline may have significant implications for the way that architecture is developed.

### 12.3.10 Capability Assessment

Before embarking upon a detailed Architecture Definition, it is valuable to understand the baseline and target capability level of the enterprise. This assessment is first carried out in Phase A and updated in Phase E.

This Capability Assessment can be examined on several levels:
- What is the capability level of the enterprise as a whole? Where does the enterprise wish to increase or optimize capability? What are the architectural focus areas that will support the desired development of the enterprise?
- What is the capability or maturity level of the IT function within the enterprise? What are the likely implications of conducting the architecture project in terms of design governance, operational governance, skills, and organization structure? What is an appropriate style, level of formality, and amount of detail for the architecture project to fit with the culture and capability of the IT organization?
- What is the capability and maturity of the architecture function within the enterprise? What architectural assets are currently in existence? Are they maintained and accurate? What standards and reference models need to be considered? Are there likely to be opportunities to create re-usable assets during the architecture project?
- Where capability gaps exist, to what extent is the business ready to transform in order to reach the target capability? What are the risks to transformation, cultural barriers, and other considerations to be addressed beyond the basic capability gap?

### 12.3.11  Change Request

Requests for Architecture Change are considered in Phase H.

During implementation of an architecture, as more facts become known, it is possible that the original Architecture Definition and requirements are not suitable or are not sufficient to complete the implementation of a solution. In these circumstances, it is necessary for implementation projects to either deviate from the suggested architectural approach or to request scope extensions. Additionally, external factors – such as market factors, changes in business strategy, and new technology opportunities – may open up opportunities to extend and refine the architecture.

In these circumstances, a Change Request may be submitted in order to request a dispensation or to kick-start a further cycle of architecture work.

### 12.3.12  Communications Plan

Enterprise architectures contain large volumes of complex and inter-dependent information. Effective communication of targeted information to the right stakeholders at the right time is a critical success factor for enterprise architecture. Development of a Communications Plan in Phase A for the architecture allows for this communication to be carried out within a planned and managed process.

### 12.3.13  Compliance Assessment

Once an architecture has been defined, it is necessary to govern that architecture through implementation to ensure that the original Architecture Vision is appropriately realized and that any implementation learnings are fed back into the architecture process. Periodic compliance reviews of implementation projects in Phase G provide a mechanism to review project progress and ensure that the design and implementation is proceeding in-line with the strategic and architectural objectives.

See Section 9.7.

### 12.3.14  Implementation and Migration Plan

The Implementation and Migration Plan provides a schedule of the projects for implementation of Target Architecture. The Implementation and Migration Plan includes executable projects grouped into managed portfolios and programs. The Implementation and Migration Strategy identifying the approach to change is a key element of the Implementation and Migration Plan.

**Development of the Implementation and Migration Plan**

The outline Implementation and Migration Plan is created in Phase E and then finalized in Phase F.

### 12.3.15  Implementation Governance Model

Once an architecture has been defined, it is necessary to plan how the Transition Architecture that implements the architecture will be governed through implementation. Within organizations that have established architecture functions, there is likely to be a governance framework already in place, but specific processes, organizations, roles, responsibilities, and measures may need to be defined on a project-by-project basis.

The Implementation Governance Model produced as an output of Phase F ensures that a project transitioning into implementation moves smoothly into appropriate Architecture Governance.

### 12.3.16  Organizational Model for Enterprise Architecture

An important deliverable of the Preliminary Phase is the Organizational Model for Enterprise Architecture.

In order for an architecture framework to be used successfully, it must be supported by the correct organization, roles, and responsibilities within the enterprise. Of particular importance is the definition of boundaries between different enterprise architecture practitioners and the governance relationships that span across these boundaries.

### 12.3.17  Request for Architecture Work

This is a document that is sent from the sponsoring organization to the architecture organization to trigger the start of an Architecture Development Cycle. Requests for Architecture Work can be created as an output of the Preliminary Phase, a result of approved architecture Change Requests, or terms of reference for architecture work originating from migration planning. In general, all the information in this document should be at a high level.

### 12.3.18  Requirements Impact Assessment

Throughout the ADM, new information is collected relating to an architecture. As this information is gathered, new facts may come to light that invalidate existing aspects of the architecture. A Requirements Impact Assessment assesses the current architecture requirements and specification to identify changes that should be made and the implications of those changes.

### 12.3.19  Solution Building Blocks

Implementation-specific building blocks from the enterprise's Architecture Repository.

See Chapter 11.

### 12.3.20  Statement of Architecture Work

The Statement of Architecture Work is created as a deliverable from Phase A and defines the scope and approach that will be used to complete an architecture development cycle. The Statement of Architecture Work is typically the document against which successful execution of the architecture project will be measured and may form the basis for a contractual agreement between the supplier and consumer of architecture services.

### 12.3.21  Tailored Architecture Framework

Selecting and tailoring a framework is the practical starting point for an architecture project.

TOGAF provides an industry standard framework for architecture that may be used in a wide variety of organizations. However, before TOGAF can be effectively used within an architecture project, tailoring at two levels is necessary.

Firstly, it is necessary to tailor the TOGAF model for integration into the enterprise. This tailoring will include integration with project and process management frameworks, customization of terminology, development of presentational styles, selection, configuration, and deployment of architecture tools, etc. The formality and detail of any frameworks adopted should also align with other contextual factors for the enterprise, such as culture, stakeholders, commercial models for enterprise architecture, and the existing level of architecture capability.

Once the framework has been tailored to the enterprise, further tailoring is necessary in order to fit the framework to the specific architecture project. Tailoring at this level will select appropriate deliverables and artifacts to meet project and stakeholder needs.

## 12.4  Summary

Architecture deliverables are the contractual or formal work products of an architecture project. The definitions provided by TOGAF are a baseline and thus a starting point for tailoring.

## 12.5  Test Yourself Questions

Q1:    Which of the following best describes the role of architecture deliverables?
    A.    They are defined so as to avoid tailoring TOGAF.
    B.    They are defined as a starting point for tailoring TOGAF.

Q2:    Which of the following acts as a holding area for all architecture-related projects within the enterprise?
    A.    Architecture Building Block
    B.    Architecture Repository
    C.    Architecture Roadmap
    D.    Architecture Vision

Q3:    Which of the following documents acts as the deliverable container for the Business, Data, Application, and Technology architectural artifacts?
    A.    Architecture Contract
    B.    Architecture Definition Document
    C.    Architecture Requirements Specification
    D.    Architecture Roadmap
    E.    Architecture Vision

Q4:   Which of the following documents is produced early in the project lifecycle and contains a summary view of the end architecture project?
   A.   Architecture Contract
   B.   Architecture Definition Document
   C.   Architecture Requirements Specification
   D.   Architecture Roadmap
   E.   Architecture Vision

Q5:   Which of the following documents is produced in Phase A as a response to the Request for Architecture Work?
   A.   Architecture Contract
   B.   Architecture Definition Document
   C.   Requirements Impact Statement
   D.   Statement of Architecture Work

## 12.6  Recommended Reading

The following are recommended sources of further information for this chapter:

- TOGAF 9 Part IV: Architecture Content Framework, Chapter 36 (Architecture Deliverables)

# Chapter 13

# TOGAF Reference Models

## 13.1 Key Learning Points

This chapter will help you understand the TOGAF Reference Models.

**Key Points Explained**

This chapter will help you to answer the following questions:

- What is the TOGAF Technical Reference Model?
- What are the characteristics of a Foundation Architecture?
- What are the basic concepts of the Integrated Information Infrastructure Reference Model (III-RM)?
- What is the relationship of the III-RM to the concept of Boundaryless Information Flow?

## 13.2 The TOGAF TRM as a Foundation Architecture

*(Syllabus Reference: Unit 12, Learning Outcome 1: You should be able to explain the role of the TRM as a Foundation Architecture.)*

A Foundation Architecture is an architecture of building blocks and corresponding standards that supports all the Common Systems Architectures, and, therefore, the complete computing environment. A Foundation Architecture is positioned at the left-hand side of the Enterprise Continuum.

TOGAF includes the Technical Reference Model (TRM) as its Foundation Architecture. The ADM explains how to develop from this generic foundation architecture to an enterprise-specific one. The TOGAF TRM describes a fundamental architecture upon which other, more specific, architectures can be based.

*(Syllabus Reference: Unit 12, Learning Outcome 2: You should be able to describe the characteristics of a Foundation Architecture.)*

Major characteristics of a Foundation Architecture include the following:

- It reflects general computing requirements.
- It reflects general building blocks.
- It defines technology standards for implementing these building blocks.
- It provides direction for products and services.
- It reflects the function of a complete, robust computing environment that can be used as a foundation.
- It provides open system standards, directions, and recommendations.
- It reflects directions and strategies.

The TRM has two main components:

1. A taxonomy that defines terminology, and provides a coherent description of the components and conceptual structure of an information system
2. A model, with an associated TRM graphic, that provides a visual representation of the taxonomy, as an aid to understanding

Figure 28 shows the high-level model of the TRM. The three main parts of the TRM (Application Software, Application Platform, and Communications Infrastructure) are connected by two interfaces (Application Platform Interface and Communications Infrastructure Interface).

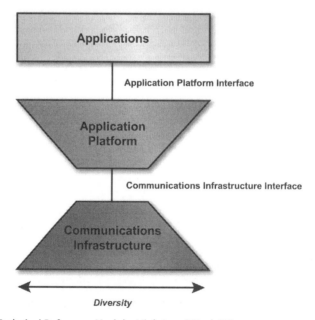

Figure 28:   Technical Reference Model – High-Level Model View

Figure 29 shows the detail of the TRM. This highlights the platform service categories (these are covered in detail in the TOGAF 9 Level 2 syllabus) together with the external environment entities, such as applications and Communications Infrastructure.

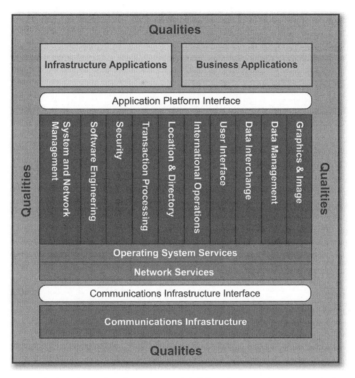

Figure 29:   Detailed Technical Reference Model (Showing Service Categories)

## 13.3  The Integrated Information Infrastructure Reference Model

*(Syllabus Reference: Unit 12, Learning Outcome 3: You should be able to briefly explain the basic concepts of the III-RM.)*

With the emergence of Internet-based technologies in recent years, for many organizations the main focus of attention, and the main return on investment in architecture effort, has shifted from the Application Platform space, modeled by the TRM, to the Application Software space. In response to this The Open Group developed the Integrated Information Infrastructure Reference Model (III-RM).

The III-RM is a reference model that focuses on the Application Software space, and is a "Common Systems Architecture" in Enterprise Continuum terms. The III-RM is a subset of the TOGAF TRM in terms of its overall scope, but it also expands certain parts of the TRM – in particular, the business applications and infrastructure applications parts – in order to provide help in addressing one of the key challenges facing the enterprise architect today: the need to design an integrated information infrastructure to enable Boundaryless Information Flow. These concepts are explained in detail below.

Like the TOGAF TRM, the III-RM has two main components:

1. A taxonomy, which defines terminology, and provides a coherent description of the components and conceptual structure of an integrated information infrastructure
2. An associated III-RM graphic, which provides a visual representation of the taxonomy, and the inter-relationship of the components, as an aid to understanding

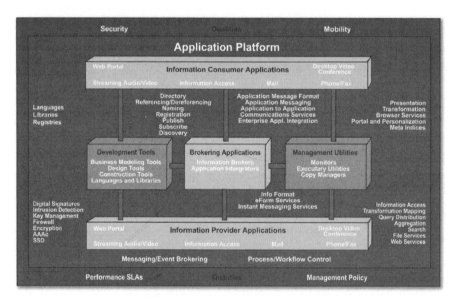

Figure 30:   III-RM High-Level View

It is fundamentally an Application Architecture reference model – a model of the application components and application services software essential for an integrated information infrastructure. It includes information provider and consumer applications, as well as brokering applications. Further detail is covered in the TOGAF 9 Certified Syllabus.

> **III-RM**
>
> The Open Group has documented the business scenario that led to the creation of the Integrated Information Infrastructure Reference Model (III-RM) in the Interoperable Enterprise Business Scenario (Doc. No. K022). This is freely available for download from the Business Scenarios section of The Open Group online bookstore at www.opengroup.org/bookstore.

## 13.4  Boundaryless Information Flow

*(Syllabus Reference: Unit 12, Learning Outcome 4: You should be able to briefly explain the relationship of the III-RM to the concept of Boundaryless Information Flow.)*

The Boundaryless Information Flow problem space is one that is shared by many customer members of The Open Group, and by many similar organizations worldwide. It is essentially the problem of getting information to the right people at the right time in a secure, reliable manner, in order to support the operations that are core to the extended enterprise.

In General Electric, Jack Welch invented the term "the Boundaryless Organization", not to imply that there are no boundaries, but that they should be made permeable.

Creating organizational structures that enabled each individual department to operate at maximum efficiency was for a long time accepted as the best approach to managing a large enterprise. Among other benefits, this approach fostered the development of specialist skills in staff, who could apply those skills to specific aspects of an overall activity (such as a manufacturing process), in order to accomplish the tasks involved better, faster, and cheaper. As each overall activity progressed through the organization, passing from department to department (for example, from Design to Production to Sales), each department would take inputs from the previous department in the process, apply its own business processes to the activity, and send its output to the next department in line.

In today's world where speed, flexibility, and responsiveness to changing markets make the difference between success and failure, this method of working is no longer appropriate. Organizations have been trying for some time to overcome the limitations imposed by traditional organization structures. Many business process re-engineering efforts have been undertaken and abandoned because they were too ambitious, while others cost far more in both time and money than originally intended.

However, organizations today recognize that they need not abandon functional or departmental organization altogether. They can enable the right people to come together in cross-functional teams so that all the skills, knowledge, and expertise can be brought to bear on any specific problem or business opportunity.

But this in turn poses its own challenges. CIOs are under enormous pressure to provide access to information to each cross-functional team on an as-required basis, and yet the sources of this data can be numerous and the volumes huge.

Even worse, the IT systems, which have been built over a period of 20 or 30 years at a cost of many billions of dollars, and are not about to be thrown out or replaced wholesale, were built for each functional department. So although it may be possible to get people to work together effectively (no minor achievement in itself), the IT systems they use are designed to support the old-style thinking. The IT systems in place today do not allow for information to flow in support of the boundaryless organization. When they do, then we will have Boundaryless Information Flow.

The Open Group's Interoperable Enterprise Business Scenario, originally published in 2001, crystallizes this need for Boundaryless Information Flow and describes the way in which this need drives IT customers' deployment of their information infrastructure.

In this scenario, the customer's problem statement says that the customer enterprise could gain significant operational efficiencies and improve the many different business processes of the enterprise – both internal processes, and those spanning the key interactions with suppliers, customers, and partners – if only it could provide staff with:

- **Integrated information** so that different and potentially conflicting pieces of information are not distributed throughout different systems
- **Integrated access to that information** so that staff can access all the information they need and have a right to, through one convenient interface

The infrastructure that enables this vision is termed the "integrated information infrastructure".

One of the key challenges for the architect in today's enterprise is to work out, and then communicate to senior management, how far technologies such as web services, application integration services, etc. can go toward achieving an integrated information infrastructure, and realizing the vision of Boundaryless Information Flow, in the enterprise concerned.

The Open Group's follow-up analysis of the Interoperable Enterprise Business Scenario has resulted in the development of an integrated information infrastructure model (the III-RM), which depicts the major components required to address the Boundaryless Information Flow problem space, and can help the architect in this task.

The III-RM thus provides insights related to customer needs for Boundaryless Information Flow in enterprise environments. The model also points to rules and standards to assist in leveraging solutions and products within the value chain.

> **Boundaryless Information Flow**
> 1. A trademark of The Open Group.
> 2. A shorthand representation of "access to integrated information to support business process improvements" representing a desired state of an enterprise's infrastructure specific to the business needs of the organization. An infrastructure that provides Boundaryless Information Flow has open standard components that provide services in a customer's extended enterprise that:
>    • Combine multiple sources of information
>    • Securely deliver the information whenever and wherever it is needed, in the right context for the people or systems using that information
>
> [Source: TOGAF 9 Part I: Introduction, Chapter 3 (Definitions)]

## 13.5  Summary

The TOGAF Technical Reference Model provides a model and core taxonomy of generic platform services. In summary:

- It is a Foundation Architecture.
- It can be used to build any system architecture.
- A taxonomy defines consistent terminology.

The III-RM is a model of the key components for developing, managing, and operating an integrated information infrastructure. In summary:

- It is an example of a Common Systems Architecture.
- The focus is on applications rather than the platform.
- It has two main components: a taxonomy and an associated graphic.
- A key driver for development of the model is the need for Boundaryless Information Flow; getting information to the right people at the right time in a secure, reliable, and timely manner.

## 13.6 Test Yourself Questions

Q1:    Which of the following is *not* a characteristic of the TOGAF
       Foundation Architecture?
       A.   It reflects general building blocks.
       B.   It defines open standards for building blocks implementation.
       C.   It provides open systems standards.
       D.   It provides guidelines for testing collections of systems.
       E.   It reflects general computing requirements.

Q2:    Which of the following best describes the purpose of the TRM?
       A.   To provide a framework for IT governance
       B.   To provide a visual model, terminology, and coherent description
            of components and structure of an information system
       C.   To provide a method for architecture development
       D.   To provide a system engineering viewpoint on a possible solution

Q3:    Where is the TOGAF Technical Reference Model positioned in terms
       of the Enterprise Continuum?
       A.   The left-hand side of the Architecture Continuum
       B.   The right-hand side of the Architecture Continuum
       C.   The left-hand side of the Solutions Continuum
       D.   The right-hand side of the Solutions Continuum

Q4:    Which of the following architecture domains does the III-RM
       describe?
       A.   Business
       B.   Data
       C.   Application
       D.   Technology

Q5:    How is the III-RM classified in terms of the Enterprise Continuum?
       A.   Industry Solution
       B.   Foundation Architecture
       C.   Common Systems Architecture
       D.   Common Systems Solution

Q6:  Which of the following was a key driver for the development of the III-RM?

A.  Boundaryless Information Flow

B.  Clinger-Cohen

C.  PRINCE2

D.  Sarbanes-Oxley

## 13.7  Recommended Reading

The following are recommended sources of further information for this chapter:

- TOGAF 9 Part VI: TOGAF Reference Models

# Answers to Test Yourself Questions

## A.1 Answers to the Test Yourself Questions

This appendix contains a table of the answers to the Test Yourself Questions organized by chapter of the Study Guide.

| Reference | Answer | Notes |
|---|---|---|
| Chapter 1 | Q1. B | There are two levels; Level 1 leads to TOGAF 9 Foundation and Level 2 leads to TOGAF 9 Certified. |
| | Q2. B | TOGAF 9 Foundation is the entry-level qualification. Options C and D do not exist as options within the program. |
| | Q3. C | These match the principles stated in the Certification Policy document. |
| | Q4. D | Guidelines for adapting the ADM: Iteration and Levels is part of the Level 2 Syllabus for the TOGAF 9 Certified qualification. It is not part of the TOGAF 9 Foundation Syllabus. |
| | Q5. B | The TOGAF 9 Part 1 Examination contains 40 questions only. |
| Chapter 2 | Q1. B | TOGAF is both an architecture framework and a method for architecture development. |
| | Q2. E | All of the reasons given are reasons for needing an architecture framework. |
| | Q3. C | The TRM, is part of the Foundation Architecture, which is contained in Part VI: TOGAF Reference Models. |
| | Q4. E | Pattern Architecture is not one of the four, which are BDAT: Business, Data, Application, and Technology Architecture. |
| | Q5. B | Part II: the ADM. |

| Reference | Answer | Notes |
|---|---|---|
| Chapter 3 | Q1. B | Phase A: Architecture Vision is the initial phase of a cycle. Note that the Preliminary Phase is a preparatory phase. |
| | Q2. D | Phase G: Implementation Governance |
| | Q3. B | Phase A: Architecture Vision |
| | Q4. B | Phase C is Information Systems Architecture. There is no Requirements Architecture, but there is a Requirements Management phase. |
| | Q5. A | Artifact |
| | Q6. D | A model for classifying artifacts. |
| | Q7. D | The Reference Library. |
| Chapter 4 | Q1. B | Foundation Architecture |
| | Q2. D | Gap is used in the context of gap analysis, where it is used to identify differences between Baseline and Target Architectures. |
| | Q3. C | The Enterprise Continuum |
| | Q4. C | Stakeholder |
| | Q5: E | Strategic Architecture |
| | Q6: E | Transition Architecture |
| Chapter 5 | Q1. D | Phase H: Architecture Change Management |
| | Q2. B | Step 9 is Create Architecture Definition Document. |
| | Q3. B | Version 0.1 indicates that a high-level outline of the architecture is in place. Typically this version is produced in the Architecture Vision phase. |
| | Q4. B | The Architecture Capability Framework is a set of best practices and guidelines and not a model that is populated as such. |
| | Q5. D | Phases are not mandatory. The ADM is recommended to be tailored, which may include omitting phases. |
| | Q6. D | Large and complex enterprises usually cannot be successfully treated as a single entity and a federated approach is recommended. |
| | Q7. C | Reference Data, Process Status, Audit Information are the recommended information areas managed by a governance repository. |
| | Q8. D | Data Architecture is not a Dimension in itself |

| Reference | Answer | Notes |
|-----------|--------|-------|
| Chapter 6 | Q1. A | It is the virtual repository of all assets produced during application of the ADM |
| | Q2. A | Deliverables from previous architecture work |
| | Q3. D | Deliverables from previous architecture work |
| | Q4. E | All of the answers apply. |
| | Q5. C | The two continua are the constituent parts. |
| | Q6. A | The III-RM is a Common Systems Architecture. |
| | Q7. D | ABBs are part of the Architecture Continuum. |
| | Q8. A | Systems libraries |
| | Q9. A | The Architecture Repository |
| | Q10. D | Reference Library |
| | Q11. A | Capability Architectures |
| | Q12. B | Standards compliance is used as part of Architecture Governance. |
| Chapter 7 | Q1. C | Phase C: Information Systems Architectures |
| | Q2. A | The Preliminary Phase |
| | Q3. B | Develop a high-level aspirational vision of the capabilities and business value to be delivered as a result of the proposed enterprise architecture |
| | Q4. A | Creation of the Architecture Vision occurs in Phase A. |
| | Q5. C | Capability Maturity models are recommended. |
| | Q6. B | Phase A commences with receipt of the Request for Architecture Work. |
| | Q7. A | Business Scenarios |
| | Q8. B | Business Architecture is undertaken first so as to demonstrate the business value of subsequent architecture work to key stakeholders. |
| | Q9. B | Business rules, job descriptions are considered relevant in Phase B. |

| Reference | Answer | Notes |
|-----------|--------|-------|
|           | Q10. C | The III-RM |
|           | Q11. A | Phase E generates the outline Implementation and Migration Strategy. |
|           | Q12. B | Phase F |
|           | Q13. C | Phase G |
|           | Q14. D | Ensure the Architecture Governance Framework is executed |
|           | Q15. C | Simplification change |
|           | Q16. A | Architecture Requirements are managed across all phases of the ADM. |
| Chapter 8 | Q1. D  | Requirements Management handles the flow of requirements. |
|           | Q2. C  | Rationale |
|           | Q3. B  | Specific |
|           | Q4. B  | Phase A when creating the Architecture Vision. |
|           | Q5. B  | If correctly eliminated you would not add it back to the target. |
|           | Q6. C  | Presentation Interoperability |
|           | Q7. E  | It is for determining the readiness of an organization to accept change. |
|           | Q8. B  | It is the residual risk after mitigating actions have been taken. |
|           | Q9. C  | It is a business planning technique focussed on business outcomes |
| Chapter 9 | Q1. B  | It is the Architecture Board that manages the activity. |
|           | Q2. A  | Expenditure control is not included. |
|           | Q3. C  | All actions and their decision support will be available for inspection. |
|           | Q4. A  | Compliance is part of process. |
|           | Q5. D  | Budgetary control is outside. |
|           | Q6. E  | These are all benefits. |
|           | Q7. A  | Resourcing |
|           | Q8. B  | The agreement is between development partners and sponsors. |
|           | Q9. C  | Where no features are in common then it is termed Irrelevant. |

| Reference | Answer | Notes |
|---|---|---|
|  | Q10. A | Architecture Board |
|  | Q11. D | Phase D: Technology Architecture |
| Chapter 10 | Q1. E | Stakeholder |
|  | Q2. A | It is the other way round; a viewpoint is considered a template for a view. |
|  | Q3. D | They are not synonymous as concerns are used to derive requirements. |
|  | Q4. E | Radio is the common tool. |
|  | Q5. B | A and C should be one or more stakeholders/concerns; D is incorrect. |
| Chapter 11 | Q1. D | Building blocks should have a loose coupling to implementation to allow for multiple implementations and re-implementation. |
|  | Q2. A | ABBs define functionality – not implementation. |
|  | Q3. D | Phase E |
| Chapter 12 | Q1. B | TOGAF should be tailored for use. |
|  | Q2. B | The Architecture Repository |
|  | Q3. B | The Architecture Definition Document |
|  | Q4. E | Architecture Vision |
|  | Q5. D | The Statement of Architecture Work |
| Chapter 13 | Q1. D | Testing guidelines are not included. |
|  | Q2. B | It is a visual model and taxonomy. |
|  | Q3. A | It is at the left-hand side, the most generic, of the Architecture Continuum. |
|  | Q4. C | It is an Application Architecture reference model. |
|  | Q5. C | It is a Common Systems Architecture. |
|  | Q6. A | The Boundaryless Information Flow problem space led to development of the III-RM. |

# Test Yourself Examination Paper

## B.1 Examination Paper

The purpose of this appendix is to provide an examination paper that will allow you to assess your knowledge of the TOGAF 9 Foundation Syllabus.

> Prior to attempting this examination paper you should have worked through this Study Guide section by section, answering the Test Yourself questions and reading the referenced sections from the TOGAF document. If you have completed your preparation, then you can then attempt this examination paper. If not, please spend some time preparing as suggested.

## B.2 Questions

The examination paper provided in this appendix uses a simple multiple-choice format, which is the same as the certification examination. Each question has one single correct answer, that scores one point.

Please read each question carefully before reading the answer options. Be aware that some questions may seem to have more than one right answer, but you are to look for the one that makes the most sense and is the most correct.

See Appendix C for the answers.

**Item 1**

Question:

Which one of the following best describes TOGAF?

A. A framework and method for architecture development
B. An architecture pattern
C. A business model
D. A method for developing Technology Architectures
E. A method for IT Governance

**Item 2**

Question:

Which part of the TOGAF document provides a number of architecture development phases, together with narratives for each phase?

A. Part I: Introduction
B. Part II: Architecture Development Method (ADM)
C. Part III: ADM Guidelines and Techniques
D. Part IV: Architecture Content Framework
E. Part V: Enterprise Continuum and Tools

**Item 3**

Question:

According to TOGAF, all of the following are suggested characteristics of an architecture framework, *except* _____

A. A common vocabulary
B. A list of recommended standards
C. A method for designing a target state of the enterprise in terms of building blocks
D. A set of structures which can be used to develop a broad range of architectures
E. A software development lifecycle method

**Item 4**

Question:

Which of the TOGAF architecture development phases includes the development of Data and Application Architectures?

A. Phase A
B. Phase B
C. Phase C
D. Phase D
E. Phase E

### Item 5

Question:

Which one of the following does the Architecture Content Framework describe as a work product that is contractually specified, formally reviewed, and signed off by the stakeholders?

A.  An artifact

B.  A building block

C.  A catalog

D.  A deliverable

E.  A matrix

### Item 6

Question:

Which of the following best completes the sentence: The Enterprise Continuum _____

A.  describes a database of open industry standards

B.  is an architecture framework

C.  is a technical reference model

D.  provides a method for architecture development

E.  provides methods for classifying artifacts

### Item 7

Question:

According to TOGAF, in which ADM phase does the initial implementation planning occur?

A.  Phase A: Architecture Vision

B.  Phase B: Business Architecture

C.  Phase C: Information Systems Architectures

D.  Phase D: Technology Architecture

E.  Phase E: Opportunities and Solutions

**Item 8**

Question:

According to TOGAF, which of the following is the reason why the first execution of an ADM cycle will be more difficult than later cycles?

A. Because management is not familiar with the ADM process

B. Because there are few architecture assets available

C. Because of lack of governance

D. Because of insufficient trained architecture practitioners

E. Because the Baseline Architecture must be fully defined across the enterprise

**Item 9**

Question:

As architecture deliverables and work products created in one ADM phase are modified by subsequent phases, how does TOGAF suggest tracking the changes?

A. Change control committee

B. Document checkpoints and journaling

C. Publish and subscribe system

D. Version numbers

E. Workflow management system

**Item 10**

Question:

Complete the sentence: The architectures that address the detailed enterprise needs and business requirements within the Architecture Continuum are known as _____

A. Strategic Architectures

B. Foundation Architectures

C. Industry Architectures

D. Common Systems Architectures

E. Organization-Specific Architectures

## Item 11

Question:

According to TOGAF, which one of the following is described as a view of the Architecture Repository and provides methods for classifying architecture and solution artifacts as they evolve?

A.  Architecture Landscape
B.  Architecture Governance Repository
C.  Enterprise Continuum
D.  Governance Log
E.  Standards Information Base

## Item 12

Question:

Which one of the following represents the detailed construction of the architectures defined in the Architecture Continuum?

A.  Architecture Building Blocks
B.  Conceptual Models
C.  Foundation Architectures
D.  Reference Models
E.  Solution Building Blocks

## Item 13

Question:

An organization has bought a large enterprise application. As a result, which of the following could be included in the organization's Solutions Continuum?

A.  A reference implementation of the Foundation Architecture
B.  A reference implementation of the Technical Reference Model for the organization
C.  Architecture Building Blocks for the organizations' Industry-Specific Architecture
D.  Detailed pricing information about the purchased products
E.  Product information for purchased products

**Item 14**

Question:

Complete the sentence: All of the following are technology-related drivers for architecture Change Requests, *except* _____

A.  asset management cost reductions
B.  new technology reports
C.  standards initiatives
D.  strategic change
E.  technology withdrawal

**Item 15**

Question:

Complete the sentence: In Phase C, when an existing application is to be replaced, the Data Architecture should _____

A.  be re-factored to align with the technology infrastructure
B.  describe how this change impacts other projects
C.  identify the data migration requirements
D.  include the application interoperability requirements
E.  estimate the effort required to overcome any issues

**Item 16**

Question:

The approach of the Preliminary Phase is about defining "where, what, why, who, and how we do architecture" in the enterprise concerned. Which one of the following statements is **NOT** correct?

A.  "Where" can be seen as scoping the enterprise concerned
B.  "Why" can be seen as the key drivers and elements in the context of the organization
C.  "Who" can be seen as defining the sponsor responsible for performing the architectural work
D.  "How" is determined by the frameworks selected and the methodologies that are going to be used

**Item 17**

Question:

In which phase of the ADM are the gap analysis results from the four architecture domains taken into account?

A. Phase E

B. Phase F

C. Phase G

D. Phase H

E. Requirements Management

**Item 18**

Question:

In Phase D, which of the following resources from the Architecture Repository should be considered in the development of the Technology Architecture?

A. Architecture Vision

B. Business rules, job descriptions

C. Implementation and Migration Plan

D. Stakeholder Map

E. TOGAF Technical Reference Model

**Item 19**

Question:

Complete the sentence: All of the following are part of the approach to the Preliminary Phase, *except* _____

A. defining the enterprise

B. identifying key drivers and elements in the organizational context

C. defining Architecture Contracts

D. defining the framework to be used

E. defining the requirements for architecture work

**Item 20**

Question:

In which phase of the TOGAF ADM do activities include assessing the dependencies, costs, and benefits of the migration projects?

A. Phase E

B. Phase F

C. Phase G

D. Phase H

E. Requirements Management

**Item 21**

Question:

Complete the sentence: Phase A is initiated upon receipt of _____

A. approval from the Chief Information Officer

B. a directive from the Chief Executive Officer

C. a Request for Architecture Work from the sponsoring organization

D. the Implementation and Migration Plan

E. the Requirements Analysis document

**Item 22**

Question:

Complete the sentence: Business Architecture is the first architecture activity undertaken since _____

A. it focuses on identifying and defining the key applications used in the enterprise

B. it provides knowledge that is a prerequisite for undertaking work in the other architecture domains

C. it defines the physical realization of an architectural solution

D. it finalizes the Architecture Vision and Architecture Definition Documents

E. it mobilizes supporting operations to support the ongoing architecture development

**Item 23**

Question:

Complete the sentence: According to TOGAF, Capability-Based Planning is _____

A.  a tactical planning technique that enhances system performance

B.  focused on technical capabilities

C.  focused on staffing and human resource management issues

D.  focused on business outcomes

E.  relevant to IT architecture

**Item 24**

Question:

In which phase of the ADM is an initial assessment of Business Transformation Readiness performed?

A.  Preliminary Phase

B.  Phase A

C.  Phase B

D.  Phase E

E.  Phase F

**Item 25**

Question:

Which of the following is defined as the risk categorization after the implementation of mitigating actions?

A.  Actual Level of Risk

B.  Initial Level of Risk

C.  Residual Level of Risk

D.  Strategic Level of Risk

**Item 26**

Question:

Which one of the statements about Architecture Principles is **NOT** correct?

A.  A good set of principles is complete.

B.  A principle is a general rule or guideline.

C.  A principle is transient and updated frequently.

D.  A principle statement should be succinct and unambiguous.

E.  They are described in a standard way.

**Item 27**

Question:

What technique does TOGAF recommend for identifying and understanding the requirements that an architecture must address?

A.  Stakeholder management
B.  Risk management
C.  Gap analysis
D.  Business scenarios
E.  Architecture principles

**Item 28**

Question:

Gap analysis is a key step in validating the architecture in Phase B: Business Architecture. Which one of the following statements is true?

A.  Gap analysis highlights services that are available
B.  Gap analysis highlights the impacts of change
C.  Gap analysis highlights services that are yet to be procured
D.  Gap analysis identifies areas where the Data Architecture needs to change
E.  Gap analysis can be used to resolve conflicts amongst different viewpoints

**Item 29**

Question:

According to TOGAF, which of the following best describes why an Architecture Board should be established?

A.  To conduct performance appraisals on the enterprise architecture team
B.  To conduct source code design reviews
C.  To ensure that new systems are introduced in a managed change process
D.  To facilitate the adoption of advanced technologies
E.  To oversee the implementation of the governance strategy

**Item 30**

Question:

TOGAF defines levels of architecture conformance. Which of the following describes a situation where some features in an architecture specification have not been implemented, but those that have are in accordance with the specification?

A.  Compliant

B.  Conformant

C.  Consistent

D.  Irrelevant

E.  Non-conformant

**Item 31**

Question:

Which Architecture Governance process ensures that regulatory requirements are being met?

A.  Business control

B.  Compliance

C.  Dispensation

D.  Environment management

E.  Policy management

**Item 32**

Question:

When applying a cycle of the ADM with the Architecture Vision to establish an Architecture Capability, which phase does TOGAF Part VII recommend defines the structure of the organization's Architecture Repository?

A.  Application Architecture

B.  Business Architecture

C.  Data Architecture

D.  Preliminary Phase

E.  Technology Architecture

**Item 33**

Question:

Views and viewpoints are used by an architect to capture or model the design of a system architecture. Which one of the following statements is true?

A.  A view is the perspective of an individual stakeholder

B.  A viewpoint is the perspective of an individual stakeholder

C.  Different stakeholders always share the same views

D.  Different stakeholders always share the same viewpoints

**Item 34**

Question:

Stakeholders and their concerns are key concepts in TOGAF. Which one of the following statements is false?

A.  Concerns are key interests that are crucially important to stakeholders.

B.  Stakeholders can be individuals, teams, or organizations.

C.  Stakeholders have key roles in, or concerns about, the system.

D.  Concerns should be SMART and have specific metrics.

**Item 35**

Question:

Which of the following is considered by TOGAF as an attribute of a good building block?

A.  A building block that is re-usable

B.  A building block meeting business needs

C.  A building block with public interfaces

D.  A building block that guides the development of solutions

E.  A building block that is product-aware

**Item 36**

Question:

Which one of the following best describes the content of an Architecture Building Block?

A.  Defined implementation

B.  Fundamental functionality

C.  Products and components used to implement the functionality

D.  Product or vendor-aware

E.  Specific functionality

**Item 37**

Question:

Which one of the following statements does **NOT** correctly describe architecture deliverables?

A.  They are consumed and produced across the ADM cycle

B.  They are defined to avoid tailoring the inputs and outputs of the ADM cycle

C.  They are typically contractual work products of an architecture project

D.  They are usually reviewed and signed off by the stakeholders

**Item 38**

Question:

What TOGAF deliverable identifies changes that are needed to the current architecture requirements and specification, and also documents the implications of change?

A.  Requirements Impact Assessment

B.  Architecture Vision

C.  Gap Analysis Results

D.  Architecture Landscape

E.  Architecture Roadmap

**Item 39**

Question:

Which of the following best describes the purpose of the TRM?

A.  To provide a generic framework for IT governance

B.  To provide a list of standards

C.  To provide a method for architecture development

D.  To provide a system engineering viewpoint on a possible solution

E.  To provide a visual model, and core terminology for generic platform services

**Item 40**

Question:

Where does the Integrated Information Infrastructure Reference Model fit in terms of the Enterprise Continuum?

A.  Common Systems Architectures

B.  Foundation Architectures

C.  Industry Architectures

D.  Organization-Specific Architectures

# Test Yourself Examination Paper Answers

This appendix contains the answers to the Examination Paper in Appendix B.

## C.1 Scoring the Examination

For each question, award yourself one point for each correct answer.

The target score for this examination is 28 points or more out of 40 (70%). Note that at the time of writing the certification examination has a pass mark lower than this examination, so if you can make the target you should be ready to take the real examination.

## C.2 Answers

### Item 1   A
This is the best answer. TOGAF is a framework - a detailed method and a set of supporting tools - for developing an enterprise architecture.

### Item 2   B
PART II: Architecture Development Method describes the TOGAF Architecture Development Method (ADM) - a step-by-step approach to developing an enterprise architecture in a number of phases.

### Item 3   E
An architecture framework is a foundational structure, or set of structures, which can be used for developing a broad range of different architectures. It should describe a method for designing a target state of the enterprise in terms of a set of building blocks, and for showing how the building blocks fit together. It should contain a set of tools and provide a common vocabulary. It should also include a list of recommended standards and compliant products that can be used to implement the building blocks.

**Item 4   C**
Phase C: Information Systems Architectures describes the development of Information Systems Architectures for an architecture project, including the development of Data and Application Architectures.

**Item 5   D**
A deliverable is a work product that is contractually specified and in turn formally reviewed, agreed, and signed off by the stakeholders. Deliverables represent the output of projects and those deliverables that are in documentation form will typically be archived at completion of a project, or transitioned into an Architecture Repository as a reference model, standard, or snapshot of the Architecture Landscape at a point in time.

**Item 6   E**
The Enterprise Continuum is a model providing methods for classifying architecture and solution artifacts as they evolve from generic Foundation Architectures to Organization-Specific Architectures. The Enterprise Continuum comprises two complementary concepts: the Architecture Continuum and the Solutions Continuum.

**Item 7   E**
Phase E: Opportunities & Solutions conducts initial implementation planning and the identification of delivery vehicles for the architecture defined in the previous phases.

**Item 8   B**
The first execution of the ADM will often be the hardest, since the architecture assets available for re-use will be relatively scarce. Even at this stage of development, however, there will be architecture assets available from external sources such as TOGAF, as well as the IT industry at large, that could be leveraged in support of the effort.

**Item 9   D**
Output is generated throughout the ADM process, and output in an early phase may be modified in a later phase. TOGAF recommends that the versioning of output is managed through version numbers. In all cases, the ADM numbering scheme is provided as an example. It should be adapted by the architect to meet the requirements of the organization and to work with the architecture tools and repositories employed by the organization.

### Item 10   E
Organization-Specific Architectures are viewed as being at the right end of the Architecture Continuum, and are the most relevant to the IT customer community, since they describe and guide the final deployment of solution components for a particular enterprise or extended network of connected enterprises.

### Item 11   C
The Enterprise Continuum provides a view of the Architecture Repository that shows the evolution of these related architectures from generic to specific, from abstract to concrete, and from logical to physical.

### Item 12   E
The Solutions Continuum defines what is available in the organizational environment as re-usable Solution Building Blocks (SBBs).

### Item 13   E
The Solutions Continuum is a population of the architecture with reference building blocks - either purchased products or built components - that represent a solution to the enterprise's business need expressed at that level.

### Item 14   D
Strategic change is a business driver.

### Item 15   C
When an existing application is replaced, there will be a critical need to migrate data (master, transactional, and reference) to the new application. The Data Architecture should identify data migration requirements and also provide indicators as to the level of transformation, weeding, and cleansing that will be required to present data in a format that meets the requirements and constraints of the target application.

### Item 16   C
"Who" is to identify the sponsor stakeholder(s) and other major stakeholders impacted by the business directive to create an enterprise architecture and determine their requirements and priorities from the enterprise, their relationships with the enterprise, and required working behaviors with each other. Note in this answer it incorrectly suggests that the sponsor performs the work.

**Item 17   A**

In Phase E the gap analysis results from all architecture domains are taken into account.

**Item 18   E**

The TOGAF TRM should be considered in the development of the Technology Architecture in Phase D.

**Item 19   C**

Architecture Contracts are prepared and issued in Phase G.

**Item 20   B**

Phase F activities include assessing the dependencies, costs, and benefits of the various migration projects.

**Item 21   C**

Phase A starts with receipt of a Request for Architecture Work from the sponsoring organization to the architecture organization.

**Item 22   B**

A knowledge of the Business Architecture is a prerequisite for architecture work in any other domain (Data, Application, Technology), and is therefore the first architecture activity that needs to be undertaken, if not catered for already in other organizational processes (enterprise planning, strategic business planning, business process re-engineering, etc.).

**Item 23   D**

Capability-Based Planning is a business planning technique that focuses on business outcomes. It focuses on the planning, engineering, and delivery of strategic business capabilities to the enterprise. It is business-driven and business-led and combines the requisite efforts of all lines of business to achieve the desired capability. Capability-Based Planning accommodates most, if not all, of the corporate business models and is especially useful in organizations where a latent capability to respond (e.g., an emergency preparedness unit) is required and the same resources are involved in multiple capabilities.

### Item 24   B

Business Transformation Readiness is first assessed in Phase A, so actions can be worked into Phases E and F in the Implementation and Migration Plan.

### Item 25   C

The risk categorization after implementation of mitigating actions is known as "Residual Level of Risk".

### Item 26   C

Principles are intended to be enduring and seldom amended.

### Item 27   D

Business scenarios are an important technique that may be used at various stages of the enterprise architecture, principally the Architecture Vision and the Business Architecture, but in other architecture domains as well, if required, to derive the characteristics of the architecture directly from the high-level requirements of the business. They are used to help identify and understand business needs, and thereby to derive the business requirements that the architecture development has to address.

### Item 28   C

A key step in validating an architecture is to consider what may have been forgotten.

### Item 29   E

A key element in a successful architecture governance strategy is a cross-organization Architecture Board to oversee the implementation of the strategy.

### Item 30   A

TOGAF describes "compliant" as a situation where some features in an architecture specification have not been implemented, but those that have are in accordance with the specification.

### Item 31   B

The Compliance process ensures regulatory requirements are being met.

**Item 32  C**

The Data Architecture would define the structure of the organization's Enterprise Continuum and Architecture Repository.

**Item 33  B**

A view is what you see. A viewpoint is where you are looking from - the vantage point or perspective that determines what you see.

**Item 34  D**

"Concerns" are the key interests that are crucially important to the stakeholders in the system, and determine the acceptability of the system. Concerns may pertain to any aspect of the system's functioning, development, or operation, including considerations such as performance, reliability, security, distribution, and evolvability. The terms "concern" and "requirement" are not synonymous. Concerns are the root of the process of decomposition into requirements. Concerns are represented in the architecture by these requirements. Requirements should be SMART (e.g., specific metrics).

**Item 35  A**

TOGAF considers re-usability an attribute of a good building block.

**Item 36  B**

An ABB has fundamental functionality and attributes: semantic, unambiguous, including security capability and manageability.

**Item 37  B**

TOGAF provides a typical baseline of architecture deliverables in order to better define the activities required in the ADM and act as a starting point for tailoring within a specific organization.

**Item 38  A**

Throughout the ADM, new information is collected relating to an architecture. As this information is gathered, new facts may come to light that invalidate existing aspects of the architecture. A Requirements Impact Assessment assesses the current architecture requirements and specification to identify changes that should be made and the implications of those changes.

**Item 39    E**

The TOGAF Foundation Architecture is an architecture of generic services and functions that provides a foundation on which more specific architectures and architectural components can be built. This Foundation Architecture is embodied within the Technical Reference Model (TRM), which provides a model and taxonomy of generic platform services.

**Item 40    A**

The TOGAF Integrated Information Infrastructure Reference Model (III-RM) is a Common Systems Architecture that focuses on the requirements, building blocks, and standards relating to the vision of Boundaryless Information Flow.

# TOGAF 9 Foundation Syllabus

This appendix provides a copy of the Level 1 Learning Units that comprise the syllabus for the TOGAF 9 Foundation certification. Each learning outcome is phrased in terms of what the candidate should have learned. The KLP[1] references can be used to trace the requirement back to sections of the TOGAF 9 document.

## D.1 Basic Concepts

| 1 | Basic Concepts |
|---|---|
| | **Purpose**<br>The purpose of this Learning Unit is to introduce the basic concepts of Enterprise Architecture and TOGAF.<br>**KLP Reference**<br>1-*, 2-*<br>**Learning Outcome**<br>The Candidate must be able to:<br>1. Describe what an enterprise is (KLP 1.2-1)<br>2. Explain the purpose of an enterprise architecture (KLP 1.2-2)<br>3. List the business benefits of having an enterprise architecture (KLP 1.2-3)<br>4. Define what an Architecture Framework is (KLP 1.2-4)<br>5. Explain why TOGAF is suitable as a framework for enterprise architecture (KLP 1.2-5)<br>6. Describe the structure of TOGAF, and briefly explain the contents of each of the parts (KLP 1.1-1, 1.1-2)<br>7. Briefly explain what TOGAF is (KLP 2.1-1)<br>8. Explain what architecture is in the context of TOGAF (KLP 2.2-1)<br>9. List the different types of architecture that TOGAF deals with (KLP 2.3-1) |

---

1  KLP is an abbreviation for Key Learning Point. A learning outcome comprises one or more key learning points.

## D.2  Core Concepts

| 2 | Core Concepts |
|---|---|
| | **Purpose**<br>The purpose of this Learning Unit is to help the Candidate explain the core concepts of TOGAF.<br>**KLP Reference**<br>2-*<br>**Learning Outcome**<br>The Candidate must be able to define and explain the following core concepts:<br>1.  The ADM: phase names and the purpose of each phase (high-level) (KLP2.4-1)<br>2.  The Architecture Content Framework: deliverables, artifacts, and building blocks (KLP 2.5-1, KLP 31.1-1)<br>3.  The Enterprise Continuum (KLP 2.6-1)<br>4.  The Architecture Repository (KLP 2.7-1)<br>5.  How to establish and maintain an enterprise Architecture Capability (KLP 2.8-1)<br>6.  Establishing the Architecture Capability as an operational entity (KLP 2.9-1)<br>7.  How to use TOGAF with other frameworks (KLP 2.10-1) |

## D.3  General Definitions

| 3 | General Definitions |
|---|---|
| | **Purpose**<br>The purpose of this Learning Unit is to help the Candidate understand the key terminology of TOGAF.<br>**KLP Reference**<br>3-*<br>**Learning Outcome**<br>The Candidate must be able to understand and explain the following definitions from Chapter 3:<br>1.  Application (KLP 3.4-1)<br>2.  Application Architecture (KLP 3.5-1)<br>3.  Architecture (KLP 3.9-1)<br>4.  Architecture Building Block (ABB) (KLP 3.10-1)<br>5.  Architecture Development Method (ADM) (KLP 3.12-1)<br>6.  Architecture Domain (KLP 3.13-1)<br>7.  Architecture Framework (KLP 3.14-1)<br>8.  Architecture Principles (KLP 3.17-1)<br>9.  Architecture Vision (KLP 3.19-1)<br>10. Baseline (KLP 3.21-1) |

| 3 | General Definitions |
|---|---|
| | 11. Building Block (KLP 3.24-1)<br>12. Business Architecture (KLP 3.25-1)<br>13. Business Governance (KLP 3.28-1)<br>14. Capability (KLP 3.30-1)<br>15. Concerns (KLP 3.34-1)<br>16. Constraint (KLP 3.35-1)<br>17. Data Architecture (KLP 3.36-1)<br>18. Deliverable (KLP 3.37-1)<br>19. Enterprise (KLP 3.38-1)<br>20. Foundation Architecture (KLP 3.42-1)<br>21. Gap (KLP 3.44-1)<br>22. Governance (KLP 3.45-1)<br>23. Information (KLP 3.46-1)<br>24. Information Technology (IT) (KLP 3.47-1)<br>25. Logical (KLP 3.50-1)<br>26. Metadata (KLP 3.51-1)<br>27. Metamodel (KLP 3.52-1)<br>28. Method (KLP 3.53-1)<br>29. Methodology (KLP 3.54-1)<br>30. Model (KLP 3.55-1)<br>31. Modeling (KLP 3.56-1)<br>32. Objective (KLP 3.57-1)<br>33. Physical (KLP 3.61-1)<br>34. Reference Model (RM) (KLP 3.66-1)<br>35. Repository (KLP 3.67-1)<br>36. Requirement (KLP 3.68-1)<br>37. Solution Architecture (KLP 3.77-1)<br>38. Solution Building Block (SBB) (KLP 3.78-1)<br>39. Stakeholder (KLP 3.80-1)<br>40. Strategic Architecture (KLP 3.82-1)<br>41. Target Architecture (KLP 3.83-1)<br>42. Technology Architecture (KLP 3.86-1)<br>43. Transition Architecture (KLP 3.87-1)<br>44. View (KLP 3.88-1)<br>45. Viewpoint (KLP 3.89-1)<br>It is expected that these definitions would be covered as part of the learning in other units. |

## D.4  Introduction to the ADM

| 4 | Introduction to the ADM |
|---|---|
| | **Purpose**<br>The purpose of this Learning Unit is to help the Candidate understand the ADM cycle, briefly explain the objective of each phase in the cycle, and how to adapt and scope the ADM for use.<br><br>**KLP Reference**<br>2-*, 5-*<br><br>**Learning Outcome**<br>The Candidate must be able to:<br>1.  Briefly describe the ADM cycle, its phases, and the objective of each phase (KLP 2.4-1, 5.2.2-1, -2, -3)<br>2.  Describe a typical set of steps, such as those for Phases B, C, and D (KLP 5.2.2-2)<br>3.  Describe the versioning convention for deliverables used in Phases A to D (KLP 5.2.2-3)<br>4.  Briefly describe the relationship between the ADM and other parts of TOGAF (Enterprise Continuum, Architecture Repository, Foundation Architecture, Supporting Guidelines and Techniques) (KLP 5.1-1)<br>5.  Explain the purpose of the supporting guidelines and techniques, and the difference between guidelines and techniques (KLP 5.1-2)<br>6.  Briefly describe the key points of the ADM cycle (KLP 5.2.1-1)<br>7.  List the main reasons why you would need to adapt the ADM (KLP 5.3-1)<br>8.  Explain the need for the ADM process to be governed (KLP 5.4-1)<br>9.  Describe the major information areas managed by a governance repository (KLP5.4-2)<br>10. Briefly explain the reasons for scoping an architecture activity (KLP 5.5-1)<br>11. List the possible dimensions for limiting the scope (KLP 5.5-2)<br>12. Briefly explain the need for an integration framework that sits above individual architectures (KLP 5.6-1) |

# D.5  Enterprise Continuum and Tools

| 5 | Enterprise Continuum and Tools |
|---|---|
| | **Purpose**<br>The purpose of this Learning Unit is to help the Candidate understand the concept of the Enterprise Continuum, its purpose, and constituent parts.<br>**KLP Reference**<br>39-\*, 41-\*, 42-\*<br>**Learning Outcome**<br>The Candidate must be able to:<br>1.  Briefly explain what the Enterprise Continuum is (KLP 39.1-1)<br>2.  Explain how it is used in organizing and developing an architecture (KLP 39.2-1)<br>3.  Explain how the Enterprise Continuum promotes re-use of architecture artifacts (KLP 39.2-2)<br>4.  Describe the constituents of the Enterprise Continuum (KLP 39.3-1)<br>5.  Explain the purpose of the Enterprise Continuum (KLP 39.3-2)<br>6.  Explain the purpose of the Architecture Continuum (KLP 39.4-3)<br>7.  List the stages of architecture evolution defined in the Architecture Continuum (KLP 39.4-4)<br>8.  Explain the purpose of the Solutions Continuum (KLP 39.4-6)<br>9.  List the stages of architecture evolution defined in the Solutions Continuum (KLP 39.4-7)<br>10. Explain the relationship between the Enterprise Continuum and the TOGAF ADM (KLP 39.5-1)<br>11. Describe the Architecture Repository (KLP 41-1)<br>12. Explain the relationship between the Enterprise Continuum and the Architecture Repository (KLP 39.1-2, 41.1-2)<br>13. Describe the classes of information held in the Architecture Repository (KLP 41.1-2)<br>14. List the three levels of the Architecture Landscape (KLP 41.2-1)<br>15. Explain the purpose of the Standards Information Base within the Architecture Repository (KLP 41.4-1) |

## D.6  ADM Phases (Level 1)

| 6 | ADM Phases (Level 1) |
|---|---|
| | **Purpose**<br>The purpose of this Learning Unit is to help the Candidate understand how each of the ADM phases contributes to the success of enterprise architecture by understanding the objectives, and the *approach* for each phase.<br>**KLP Reference**<br>6-*, 7-*,8-*,9-*,10-*,11-*,12-*,13-*,14-*,15-*,16-*,17-*<br>**Learning Outcome**<br>**Preliminary Phase:** The Candidate must be able to:<br>1.  Describe the objectives of the phase (KLP 6.1-1)<br>2.  Briefly explain the seven aspects of the approach undertaken in this phase (KLP 6.2-1):<br>  a.  Defining the enterprise<br>  b.  Identifying key drivers and elements in the organizational context<br>  c.  Defining the requirements for architecture work<br>  d.  Defining the architecture principles that will inform any architecture work<br>  e.  Defining the framework to be used<br>  f.  Defining the relationships between management frameworks<br>  g.  Evaluating the enterprise architecture maturity<br>**Phase A:** The Candidate must be able to:<br>1.  Describe the main objectives of the phase (KLP 7.1-1)<br>2.  Briefly explain the two main aspects to the approach in this phase (KLP 7.2-1):<br>  — Creating the Architecture Vision<br>  — Business scenarios<br>**Phase B:** The Candidate must be able to:<br>1.  Describe the main objectives of the phase (KLP 8.1-1)<br>2.  Briefly explain the main aspects of the approach in this phase (KLP 8.2-1):<br>  — Developing the Baseline Description<br>  — Business modeling<br>  — Using the Architecture Repository<br>**Phase C:** The Candidate must be able to:<br>1.  Describe the main objectives of the phase (KLP 9.1-1, 10.1-1, 11.1-1)<br>2.  Briefly explain the approach recommended by TOGAF, including:<br>  — Key considerations for Data Architecture (KLP 10.2-1)<br>  — Using the Architecture Repository (KLP 10.2-1, 11.2-1)<br>**Phase D:** The Candidate must be able to:<br>1.  Describe the main objectives of the phase (KLP 12.1-1)<br>2.  Briefly explain the approach to the phase (KLP 12.2-1), including:<br>  — Using the Architecture Repository<br>**Phase E:** The Candidate must be able to:<br>1.  Describe the main objectives of the phase (KLP 13.1-1)<br>2.  Briefly explain the approach to the phase (KLP 13.2-1) |

| 6 | ADM Phases (Level 1) |
|---|---|

**Phase F:** The Candidate must be able to:
1. Describe the main objectives of the phase (KLP 14.1-1)
2. Briefly explain the approach to the phase (KLP 14.2-1)

**Phase G:** The Candidate must be able to:
1. Describe the main objectives of the phase (KLP 15.1-1)
2. Briefly explain the approach to the phase (KLP 15.2-1)

**Phase H:** The Candidate must be able to:
1. Describe the main objectives of the phase (KLP 16.1-1)
2. Briefly explain the approach to the phase (KLP 16.2-1), including:
   — Drivers for change
   — Enterprise architecture management process
   — Guidelines for maintenance versus architecture redesign

**ADM Architecture Requirements Management:** The Candidate must be able to:
1. Briefly explain how Requirements Management fits into the ADM cycle (KLP 17.1-1)
2. Describe the nature of the Requirements Management process (KLP 17.1-2)
3. Describe the approach to Requirements Management (KLP 17.2-1)

# D.7 ADM Guidelines and Techniques

| 7 | ADM Guidelines and Techniques |
|---|---|

**Purpose**

The purpose of this Learning Unit is to introduce the Candidate to the ADM Guidelines and Techniques available to support application of the ADM.

**KLP Reference**

18-*, 23-*,26-*,27-*,29-*,30-*,31-*,32-*

**Learning Outcome**

The Candidate must be able to:
1. Briefly explain the contents of Part III of TOGAF 9 (KLP 18.1-1)
2. Briefly explain the need for architecture principles and where they are used within TOGAF (KLP 23.1-1)
3. Describe the standard template for architecture principles (KLP 23.3-1)
4. Explain what makes a good architecture principle (KLP 23.4-2)
5. Understand what a business scenario is and its purpose (KLP26.1-1)
6. Explain where business scenarios are used within the ADM cycle (KLP 26.1-2)
7. Explain the purpose of gap analysis (KLP 27.2-1)
8. Describe the gap analysis technique (KLP 27.2-1)
9. Explain the term interoperability (KLP 29.2-1)
10. Understand the use of interoperability requirements within the TOGAF ADM (KLP 29.1-1)
11. Understand the Business Transformation Readiness program (KLP 30.1-2)

| 7 | ADM Guidelines and Techniques |
|---|---|
|   | 12. Understand where Business Transformation Readiness is used within the ADM (KLP 30.1-1)<br>13. Understand the characteristics of risk management (KLP 31.1-2)<br>14. Understand where risk management is used within the TOGAF ADM (KLP 31.1-1)<br>15. Understand Capability-Based Planning (KLP 32.1-1) |

## D.8  Architecture Governance (Level 1)

| 8 | Architecture Governance (Level 1) |
|---|---|
|   | **Purpose**<br>The purpose of this Learning Unit is to help the Candidate understand how Architecture Governance contributes to the Architecture Development Cycle.<br>**KLP Reference**<br>46-*, 47-*, 48-*, 49-*, 50-*<br>**Learning Outcome**<br>The Candidate must be able to:<br>1. Briefly explain the concept of Architecture Governance (KLP 50.1-1)<br>2. Describe the main concepts that make up an Architecture Governance framework (KLP 50.2-1)<br>3. Explain why Architecture Governance is beneficial (KLP 50.3-1)<br>4. Briefly explain the need for establishment of an Architecture Board (KLP 47.1-1)<br>5. List the responsibilities of an Architecture Board (KLP 47.2-1)<br>6. Briefly explain the role of Architecture Contracts (KLP 49.1-1)<br>7. Briefly explain the meaning of Architecture Compliance (KLP 48.2-1)<br>8. Briefly explain the need for Architecture Compliance (KLP 48.1-1)<br>9. Briefly explain the purpose of Architecture Compliance Reviews (KLP 48.3-1)<br>10. Briefly describe the Architecture Compliance Review process (KLP 48.4-1)<br>11. Briefly explain how the ADM can be used to establish an Architecture Capability (KLP 46.1-1) |

## D.9  Architecture Views, Viewpoints, and Stakeholders

| 9 | Architecture Views, Viewpoints, and Stakeholders |
|---|---|
| | **Purpose** |
| | The purpose of this Learning Unit is to help the Candidate understand the concepts of views and viewpoints, and their role in communicating with stakeholders as well as applying them to the Architecture Development Cycle. |
| | **KLP Reference** |
| | 35-* |
| | **Learning Outcome** |
| | The Candidate must be able to: |
| | 1. Define and explain the following key concepts (KLP 35.1-1): |
| |    — Stakeholders |
| |    — Concerns |
| |    — Views |
| |    — Viewpoints |
| | 2. Describe a simple example of a viewpoint and view (KLP 35.1-2) |
| | 3. Discuss the relationship between stakeholders, concerns, views, and viewpoints (KLP 35.1-3) |
| | 4. Describe the view creation process (KLP 35.2-1) |

## D.10  Building Blocks

| 10 | Building Blocks |
|---|---|
| | **Purpose** |
| | The purpose of this Learning Unit is to help the Candidate understand the concept of building blocks within TOGAF. |
| | **KLP Reference** |
| | 37-*, 25-* |
| | **Learning Outcome** |
| | The Candidate must be able to: |
| | 1. Define what a building block is, and explain what makes a good building block (KLP 37.2-1) |
| | 2. Explain the distinction between Architecture Building Blocks and Solution Building Blocks (KLP 37.2-2) |
| | 3. Briefly explain the use of building blocks in the ADM cycle (KLP 37.3-1) |
| | 4. Describe the characteristics of an Architecture Pattern (KLP 25.1-1) |

## D.11 ADM Deliverables

| 11 | ADM Deliverables |
|----|------------------|
| | **Purpose**<br>The purpose of this Learning Unit is to help the Candidate understand key deliverables of the ADM cycle.<br>**KLP Reference**<br>36.1-1, KLP 36.2-1<br>**Learning Outcome**<br>The Candidate must be able to:<br>1. Briefly explain the role of architecture deliverables across the ADM cycle (KLP 36.1-1)<br>2. Briefly explain the purpose of the following deliverables (KLP 36.2-1):<br>   — Architecture Building Blocks<br>   — Architecture Contract<br>   — Architecture Definition Document<br>   — Architecture Principles<br>   — Architecture Repository<br>   — Architecture Requirements Specification<br>   — Architecture Roadmap<br>   — Architecture Vision<br>   — Business Principles, Business Goals, and Business Drivers<br>   — Capability Assessment<br>   — Change Request<br>   — Communications Plan<br>   — Compliance Assessment<br>   — Implementation and Migration Plan<br>   — Implementation Governance Model<br>   — Organizational Model for Enterprise Architecture<br>   — Request for Architecture Work<br>   — Requirements Impact Assessment<br>   — Solution Building Blocks<br>   — Statement of Architecture Work<br>   — Tailored Architecture Framework<br>It is expected that at least some of these deliverables would be covered as part of the learning in other units. |

## D.12  TOGAF Reference Models (Level 1)

| 12 | TOGAF Reference Models (Level 1) |
|----|----------------------------------|
|    | **Purpose** |
|    | The purpose of this Learning Unit is to introduce the TOGAF Reference Models. |
|    | **KLP Reference** |
|    | 43-*, 44-* |
|    | **Learning Outcome** |
|    | The Candidate must be able to: |
|    | 1.  Explain the role of the TRM as a Foundation Architecture (KLP 43.1-2, 43.3-1) |
|    | 2.  Describe the major characteristics of a Foundation Architecture (KLP 43.1-1) |
|    | 3.  Briefly explain the basic concepts of the III-RM (KLP 44.1-1) |
|    | 4.  Briefly explain the relationship of the III-RM to the concept of Boundaryless Information Flow (KLP 44.1-2) |

## D.13  TOGAF Certification Program

| 13 | TOGAF Certification Program (Non-examinable) |
|----|----------------------------------------------|
|    | **Purpose** |
|    | The purpose of this Learning Unit is to help the Candidate understand the TOGAF Certification program. |
|    | **Learning Outcome** |
|    | The Candidate must be able to: |
|    | 1.  Explain the TOGAF Certification program, and distinguish between the levels for certification |

# Index

5087199R00140

Printed in Great Britain
by Amazon.co.uk, Ltd.,
Marston Gate.